JEREMY BROOKS

HEAVEN'S
MORNING BREAKS

Sensitive and practical reflections
on funeral practice

Augsburg Books
MINNEAPOLIS

HEAVEN'S MORNING BREAKS
Sensitive and practical reflections on funeral practice

© Copyright 2013 Jeremy Brooks.

Original edition published in English under the title HEAVEN'S MORNING BREAKS by Kevin Mayhew Ltd, Buxhall, England.

This edition published in 2020 by Fortress Press. All rights reserved. Except for brief quotations in critical articles or reviews, no part of this book may be reproduced in any manner without prior written permission from the publisher. Email copyright@augsburgfortress.org or write to Permissions, Fortress Press, PO Box 1209, Minneapolis, MN 55440-1209.

Unless stated otherwise, Scripture quotations are taken from *The New Revised Standard Version of the Bible*, copyright © 1989 Division of Christian Education of the National Council of the Churches of Christ in the USA. Used by permission. All rights reserved.

Cover image: © iStock 2020: Grass pasture on sunset sky and sun background stock photo by undefined
Cover design: Emily Drake

Print ISBN: 978-1-5064-6000-0

Contents

Dedication	4
About the author	5
Foreword	7

Part 1: In life, in death, O Lord

Chapter 1: Funerals are a-changing	11
Chapter 2: Whatever happened to death?	31
Chapter 3: Comfort one another with these words	43
Chapter 4: A time to speak	55
Chapter 5: Psalms, hymns and not so spiritual songs	69
Chapter 6: The symbols of death and life	81
Chapter 7: The funerals we all dread	95
Chapter 8: The death of children	105
Chapter 9: When the day is over – pastoral care for the bereaved	117

Part 2: Resources

Introduction	129
Bible readings	131
Hymns	137
Other music	143
Prayers	147
Other readings	159
Readings for annual services of remembrance	171

Part 3: Suggested orders of service

Suggested order of service for a funeral	177
Suggested order of service for a child's funeral	185
Suggested order of service for a vigil	189
Suggested order of service for an individual memorial service	193
Suggested order of service for the interment of ashes	197
Suggested order for an annual memorial service	201

Bibliography	205

Dedication

*For Dorothy with whom I have walked the journey
and who has pointed to the light.
And for our children: Ethan and Dana,
who remind me of the joy of living,
and Matthew, for whom heaven's morning has already broken.*

About the author

Jeremy Brooks is a parish priest in the Church of England. He recently completed a doctorate at Kings College London in which he looked at the changing nature of funeral ministry in the Church of England over the last twenty years.

He is married to Dorothy, who is also ordained and works as a hospital chaplain at a leading children's hospital, and they live with their two children in Buckinghamshire.

Foreword

When I was training to be a parish priest at theological college in the 1990s, there was a two-day short course at the end of our final year on taking funerals. We had had some other training in pastoral skills such as counselling, which could be considered useful, but the actual realities of taking funerals were left to a few weeks before we were actually likely to do one.

The reality for many of us was that, having started as curates, we could easily have taken three or four funerals each week from the time we started. Stories abounded of curates whose training vicars went away on holiday two weeks after they started and whilst they were away, the curate ended up taking about eight funerals! It felt like something for which we were totally unprepared at theological college.

I have always had the suspicion that funerals have not been taken as seriously as they should be by the training authorities. Certainly, in the Church of England, there has been an assumption that its clergy would carry out the majority of funeral services, and as we did not need to compete with others for business, it did not matter if they were not done too well. But that world has changed, as this book explains and it should always matter that we offer the best service that we are able to.

The other thing that I have noticed about funerals is that many parish priests find them one of the most rewarding aspects of ministry, even whilst they can appear to be of marginal importance to the church authorities. Get a group of parish clergy together and it doesn't take long before they are swapping funeral stories! Many people find this slightly surprising and worry that it sounds a little morbid, but to me, it simply reflects a healthy respect for life and death – and the privilege that we have at a time of real need in a person's life, to offer some hope.

As this book makes clear, there have been major changes in the last twenty years or so in the way that funerals are taken in Britain. No longer is it assumed that they will be conducted chiefly by church ministers, and, like baptisms and weddings, I fear that our role will become increasingly marginal. There can be a perception that church ministers will not allow all that a family will want to give thanks for a loved one's life and I felt it important to explore this fully in this book. I believe strongly that a family's desire to give thanks for a person's life and to call to mind specific memories, play particular music, or hear readings which had significance for the person who has died is in no way incompatible with the gospel. Our task is, having heard the story of this person's life, to tell the story of our Saviour's life and the meaning that can be found in that life and death in the midst of this life and death.

I would like to thank a number of people. A number of the themes of this book have been explored as part of the doctoral studies course that I have recently undertaken at Kings College London and I would like to thank my supervisors, first Dr James Steven, and then Professor Alister McGrath for their help and encouragement.

Thanks to Kevin Mayhew for inviting me to write this book, and to those who work at Kevin Mayhew Ltd for their support and encouragement along the way. I would also like to thank the congregations of the Beaconsfield Team Ministry, in particular at St Mary & All Saints, for allowing their Team Rector time for writing alongside the other pressures of parish ministry.

Finally, I should thank my wife, Dorothy Moore Brooks. She has contributed the chapter on the death of children – and indeed suggested the book's title – but has also given so much more. I am aware that so often when things have gone right for me in ministry, it is because she has pointed me in the right direction and this has been particularly true in pastoral ministry and in the ministry surrounding the time of death. I dedicate this book to her, and to our children, in thanksgiving.

Part 1
In life, in death, O Lord

Chapter 1: Funerals are a-changing
Chapter 2: Whatever happened to death?
Chapter 3: Comfort one another with these words
Chapter 4: A time to speak
Chapter 5: Psalms, hymns and not so spiritual songs
Chapter 6: The symbols of death and life
Chapter 7: The funerals we all dread
Chapter 8: The death of children
Chapter 9: When the day is over – pastoral care for the bereaved

One
Funerals are a-changing

There are certain moments in history which remain so vivid in people's imaginations that those who lived through them can always tell you where they were when the news broke. Those who remember the early 1960s will always be able to tell you where they were when they heard that President Kennedy had been shot; the impact of that assassination was enormous, not just in the USA but throughout the world. No doubt, the outbreak of World War II in 1939 had a similar impact, and, more recently, the Fall of the Berlin Wall in November 1989.

The death of Princess Diana on 31 August 1997 had a similar impact. The news broke early on the Sunday morning. I had been ordained two months previously in St Paul's Cathedral and was settling into a new life as the curate in a parish in Highgate, North London. That Sunday morning, I heard a few words on the radio before hurrying off to the 8am Communion service in my new church. A number of the worshippers had not heard the news so wondered why we included prayers for Princess Diana and Dodi Fayed amongst those who had died.

Many commentators felt that the events that followed Diana's death were some of the most extraordinary that had been witnessed in modern times in Britain, as hundreds of thousands of people poured into London to pay their respects. It felt as though time was suspended and no other news took place in Britain that week. Outside Buckingham Palace was laid a carpet of floral tributes; thousands of people came to lay flowers at the gates. This was something that was relatively new in Britain. If someone died in a road accident, flowers were sometimes left at the scene of the accident, but Diana's death brought this practice to the attention of us all.

However, it is Diana's funeral that has had the biggest impact in this country in the years since she died. Many funeral directors in Britain today would say that a huge change happened almost overnight as a result of the service held in Westminster Abbey the following Saturday, 6 September. It is estimated that some 2.5 billion people around the world watched parts of the service.

Paul Sheppy, a Baptist minister who has written a number of books on modern funeral rites, has said that three key moments from that funeral stick in people's minds:[1]

---

1. See his book *Death Liturgy and Ritual, Vol 1: A Pastoral and Liturgical Theology,* Aldershot: Ashgate, 2003, p.101.

- Elton John singing a reworking of his song 'Candle in the wind'. This had originally been written to celebrate the life of Marilyn Monroe who had similarly died young in tragic circumstances. Following Diana's death, there was huge public pressure on the singer, a friend of Princess Diana, to rewrite the song in time for the funeral service. He renamed the song 'Goodbye England's Rose' and sang it as part of the service.
- The personal tribute that was paid by Earl Spencer, Princess Diana's brother. In his speech, Earl Spencer was critical of the Royal Family – criticism which reflected the mood of many in the nation who felt that the Queen should have shown more emotion and returned from Balmoral where she had been on holiday with her family as soon as the news broke. The film *The Queen*, released in 2006 and starring Helen Mirren, portrays well the events leading up to the funeral and Queen Elizabeth's role in it.
- The singing of 'Song for Athene' by the British composer Sir John Tavener as the coffin was carried out of the Abbey. Tavener, an Orthodox Christian, used various words of Scripture and ancient funeral liturgies in the song, interspersed with long, slow alleluias.

Sheppy comments wryly that the Archbishop of Canterbury's prayers felt a bit like an intrusion into a show business event! Many clergy, who have conducted funerals for families insistent on their own input and music and want the minimum possible input from clergy, will sympathise!

So what was it about Diana's funeral that had such a big impact on the way funerals have been conducted in Britain since? Firstly, the tribute by Earl Spencer suggested to people that they did not just need to use the vicar to speak at the funeral. In the vast majority of funerals, the family, let alone the deceased, have never even met the conducting minister, so there can be a feeling that the service is not very personal. Ken Livingstone, the former Mayor of London, once memorably complained that Church of England funerals were about as moving as a supermarket checkout queue! Since 1997, it has become much more usual for a tribute to be given by a family member or friend, with the hope that it will be more moving and individual for the person who has died.

Secondly, the use of Elton John's song gave permission for people to include their own favourite piece of music in a funeral service. If Westminster Abbey could cope with the singing of a pop song in church, there seemed to be little reason why parish churches all over the country could not allow the same thing. Of course, it is sometimes too much to expect that there will be live singing but, with the increasing use of good sound systems in churches and in cemetery and crematorium chapels, the technology is available for recorded music to be used as an integral part of the service.

Although people remember Tavener's music, it has not had the same impact in terms of funerals. The music is haunting and moving; it is noticeable how many families prefer music now which is more cheerful!

This chapter will outline three main areas of change that have taken place in funeral practice over the last 20 years. These changes are not just as a result of Diana's death, though that has been a key factor. It is important to ask, right at the beginning of the book, whom the funeral is for; if we know the answer to that question, it might affect how it should be conducted and what to include.

Changes in funeral practices in Britain
1. Changes in venues for funerals

Over the last century, we have seen a change in this country from a time when everyone was buried to a situation today when most people are cremated. Previously, most funeral services happened in the town or village where the person lived; now, most take place exclusively at the crematorium, which may well be a few miles or more from the person's home.

The first crematoria in this country were opened in 1901 in Hull and the following year in Golders Green, North London. By 1968 there were more cremations in Britain than burials, and by 1988 about 70 per cent of all deaths were dealt with by cremation. This figure has remained fairly constant since. In a series of debates between 1937 and 1944, the Church of England held that there was no theological significance to be attached to the means of disposal of a corpse as God is as capable of raising new resurrection bodies from the ashes of fire as from the dust of the earth. In 1963, the Pope declared that it was no longer illegal for Roman Catholic priests to conduct cremations.

It is often assumed in this country that cremation would be a better solution because of the lack of space: cremated remains do not take up as much space as a buried body. However, a brief look at the practices in other countries would suggest that space is not a critical factor. In Canada, the second largest country in the world, and one of the most sparsely populated, the majority of the population favour cremation over burial. In neighbouring USA, with its much greater population, only a third of deaths are currently dealt with by cremation. In Belgium, a country with a similar density of population to England, though with a much smaller land mass, most people are still buried. However, in that country, unlike the UK, the regular reuse of graves after a suitable interval for a new body is commonplace. It is generally accepted that once a body has decomposed, there is nothing to prevent the reuse of the grave.

The change of venue for funeral services away from a church has happened most markedly in the last 20 years. When most crematoria were built, it was assumed that a service would take place in church first and that the crematorium would only deal with the committal part of the service. Crematoria chapels tended to be fairly small because it was assumed that many who had attended the funeral service would not go on to the cremation – it would be for close family and friends only. Because the committal part of the service is fairly quick and need not take more than five or ten minutes, timings of funerals at the crematorium were limited to 30 minutes, or even less. Conducting ministers would be advised not to exceed 20 minutes for the service, as there would be another family waiting for the next service.

However, it has become increasingly common for the whole funeral service to be conducted at the crematorium. In my local crematorium, fewer than 20 per cent of the services are committals only, preceded or followed by a full service in church; the rest are wholly carried out at the crematorium. Many crematoria have responded well to this change by increasing the time between services from 30 to 45 minutes, and some have built new, bigger chapels to cope with the demand.

One of the consequences of this, of course, is that funerals are increasingly conducted away from the community of which the deceased person was a part and carried out in a municipal building some distance away. Most religious services in England used to be conducted by clergy from the Church of England, central to which is the parish system. This means that, wherever you live in England, you live in a particular parish and are able to use the parish church for key events in your life, such as having a child baptised, getting married, or your funeral. It is not dependent on being a member of the church, or even believing anything for which the church stands; it is enough that you live in that parish.

As far as funerals are concerned, this meant that even if death had occurred at a distance – in the district general hospital several miles away, or further even afield – the funeral itself would be held in the heart of the community where the person lived. Where the whole service takes place at a crematorium several miles away, this is no longer true.

Although cremation has become the most popular form of committal, it is worth considering the alternatives for families. In the UK, still a little over a quarter of the population are currently buried on death, and this figure has remained fairly constant over the last 25 years. This contrasts with the previous 20 years which saw a big drop in burial rates.

With the rise of ecological awareness and the green movement in this country, concern has been expressed about the environmental impact of cremation. The energy required to heat the crematorium ovens to up to 1000°C is considerable, and many wonder whether there is a more environmentally friendly alternative. 'Green burials' are now increasingly common, and there are now more natural burial grounds in this country than there are crematoria, although they still only account for a very small proportion of all services carried out.

The first woodland burial site was opened in Carlisle in 1993 in response to the lack of space in cemeteries. According to the Association of Natural Burial Grounds,[2] there are now some 260 such sites, either exclusively for natural burial or as an area within a larger cemetery. With some sites, a tree is planted in place of a headstone in memorial of the person who has died; in other sites, the person is buried among trees already grown and, while there will be a temporary marker for the grave, it is not anticipated that this will endure beyond a year or two.

Alternatives to burial and cremation are being considered. One of these is resomation, where the body is placed in a solution of water and potassium hydroxide and effectively dissolved. Another is promession, in which the body is freeze dried before being buried in a shallow grave. Both these processes claim to be far more environmentally friendly than traditional means of disposal, but licences have not yet been granted in this country.

2. Change in content of funerals

One of the most influential books written in the last 25 years on how to conduct a funeral was called *Funerals and How to Improve Them* by Tony Walter,[3] a sociologist who is now working as a professor at the Centre for Death and Society at the University of Bath. He was unhappy about how impersonal funerals were then: they were often conducted by the crematorium 'duty minister' who had never known the deceased and had only met the family at the door to the crematorium chapel. It was not unusual to hear complaints from crematorium staff about clergy who appeared to forget the name of the person whose funeral they were conducting, and there was no space for any personal information to be given as part of the service. Given that the duty minister may well have had six or seven services to conduct that day, it was hardly surprising that he could not include personal details about the deceased.

---

2. The ANBG was formed by the Natural Death Centre and details can be found on their website at www.naturaldeath.org.uk (accessed 16 April 2013).
3. Tony Walter, *Funerals and How to Improve Them*, London: Hodder & Stoughton, 1990.

This is a far cry from the way most funerals are conducted today. The practice of 'crem duty' has all but disappeared from this country, and anyone conducting a funeral service would attempt to visit family members in order to plan the service together, or at least have a telephone call or email conversation in which personal facts about the person's life would be gleaned.

Tony Walter's concern was that funerals should be 'person centred'. In other words, the content of the funeral should be dictated not by the words of a liturgy of the faith official conducting the service, but by the life of the person who had died. There should be space for personal tributes or particular pieces of music that were significant for that person, alongside the religious content of the funeral that shaped the overall service. When he wrote the book in 1990, Walter pointed to Melbourne, Australia, as a place where such things were already happening. Today there would be no need to go beyond the shores of this country to find examples of how it can be done.

One of the most popular pieces of music that is played at funeral services today is Frank Sinatra's 'My way'. Most clergy groan when the family suggest that they would like their loved one to go out to this piece: it does feel as though nothing could be further from the Christian gospel of grace. In place of a recognition of God's overwhelming love which resulted in him laying down his life on behalf of others is the proud assertion of Ol' Blue Eyes that he got to the end of his life and did it 'my way'. Nonetheless, 'My way' does seem to be an eloquent symbol of the way in which funerals are conducted today. Writing a few years after *Funerals and How to Improve Them*, Walter describes this as 'the Sinatra syndrome' in which 'it is not so much that I have decided to do it my way; I am required to.'[4]

Although many ministers may resist items such as 'My way' at Christian funerals, there has been a big increase in the use of popular music alongside sung hymns. It is quite usual for a family to choose a particular piece of music as the congregation is coming into the church or chapel, and similarly to play something suitable as they leave at the end. Indeed, it can also be helpful to suggest to the family that they could listen to another track during the course of the service; where a service is full of the spoken word, sometimes to have a break from that with the playing of music can aid enormously the flow of the service and its impact on the mourners.

The reservations that many clergy have about pieces of music like 'My way' highlights the dilemma that faces ministers conducting funerals today. On the one hand, they see a funeral as an important opportunity to offer the love of God and proclaim the saving hope of

---

4. Tony Walter, *The Revival of Death*, London: Routledge, 1994, p.37.

Jesus' death and resurrection. On the other hand, the chief concern for the family is to remember their loved one and look back on his or her life with thanksgiving. To refuse to allow the family a cherished desire at a funeral may obscure the love of God far more effectively than allowing a piece of music which doesn't accord with our own theology. There is undoubtedly a tightrope to be walked in agreeing the content of a funeral – one that neither falls over into uncaring Christian dogmatism nor falls into individualistic notions of life's purpose and the afterlife that owe little to historic Christianity.

It is not just in musical items that the family can make the service unique to the person who has died; individual tributes are now commonplace, as are poems and readings taken from a wide variety of sources. These will be considered later in Chapter 3: suffice at this stage to say that the concern to balance the Christian gospel with the hopes and wishes of the family is as important here as it is with regard to musical items.

3. The official conducting the service

The biggest change that has taken place over the last decade in the way funerals are conducted is with regard to the person who actually takes the service. As late as the 1990s, it was assumed that the vast majority of funeral services would be conducted by a religious minister. It was possible to have a humanist service in which all religious references were excluded, but they accounted for less than 1 per cent of all funerals conducted. Clearly, in parts of the country with a large immigrant population – particularly from the Asian subcontinent – a significant number of funerals were conducted by their religious leaders. For the rest of the population, unless their family heritage was Roman Catholic or Orthodox, or they were members of a non-conformist church, their service would be conducted by a Church of England minister.[5] In 1998, in a Church of England General Synod debate, it was estimated that its clergy conducted about 70 per cent of all funerals in this country. This was seen as evidence that the nation was still basically Christian. Although fewer and fewer people went to church or claimed any religious affiliation, the fact that their funeral would be conducted by a Christian minister gave the Church succour against its opponents who claimed that the church was dying in this country. The picture is not nearly so clear cut today.

In January 2002, the Government published a White Paper entitled *Civil Registration: Vital Change*. This paved the way for professionals

---

5. I am referring here to the situation in England. In Wales, the Church in Wales, which is also part of the Anglican Communion, is the state church and would carry out most services. In Scotland, the established church is the Presbyterian Church of Scotland, and its ministers would do most of the funerals.

other than church officials to start conducting funerals. In 2004, the Institute of Civil Funerals was formed by Anne Barber. Its website states that its purpose is to offer funerals that are 'driven by the wishes, beliefs and values of the deceased and their family, not by the beliefs and ideology of the person conducting the funeral.'[6]

Tony Walter's key phrase of offering 'person-centred' funerals accords well with this mission statement: the funeral should be about the person who has died, not about proclaiming a set of beliefs such as Christianity, or indeed an ideology such as humanism, with which the deceased may have been equally uncomfortable.

As a result of the 2002 White Paper, a new profession of civil funeral celebrants sprang into being. These celebrants now conduct a significant proportion of funerals in this country. In 2009, The Co-operative Funeralcare carried out research into the 100,000 funerals it conducts each year and calculated that about 25 per cent of these were led by a civil celebrant.[7]

There are many benefits that a civil celebrant can bring to a funeral. For many such celebrants, this is their only job so they take a great deal of time and care to ensure that the service reflects the wishes of the family. At the end of the service the family is given a copy of the whole order. Even many celebrants who have no other paid employment will only aim to conduct two or three funerals a week so that they can take the care that is needed to meet the family's needs. Most people in this country do not describe themselves as religious, yet many still want to be able to say the Lord's Prayer, listen to a recording of *Ave Maria* or even sing 'The Lord's my shepherd'. Because the philosophy of civil celebrants is centred on the deceased's beliefs and values, they will normally allow such items.

A humanist, by contrast, would exclude any religious music and readings. In a conversation I had recently with a local funeral director, he commented that it was often difficult to tell the difference between services conducted by civil celebrants and those led by church ministers, such is the high level of religious content used by the former group.

There are some dilemmas, however, in the use of civil celebrants. There are a number of professional bodies, including the Institute of Civil Funerals, to which civil celebrants can belong, although many celebrants do not belong to any such organisation. In 2010, IoCF members conducted some 4000 funerals. Even comparing this figure against the 25,000 celebrant-led services conducted for the Co-op, let alone for any other funeral director, makes it clear how many other services are conducted by celebrants not affiliated to a professional

---

6. www.iocf.org.uk (accessed 16 April 2013).
7. *The ways we say goodbye*, available at http://www.co-operative.coop/Funeralcare/brochures/march2013/The-way-we-say-goodbye/ (accessed 29 April 2013).

body. If a funeral is carried out badly, to whom can the family complain? Given how vulnerable grieving families are at this time, it is important that they are protected from people who might trample on their vulnerability. This is not to deny that a church minister could be equally insensitive in the conduct of the service; simply that there is an avenue of recourse if that proves to be the case.

Training is also key; a kind nature and the ability to use words well are not enough. Again, good training is offered by the IoCF and other organisations such as Green Fuse, but it is not a prerequisite.

At the time of writing, it is still true that most funerals are conducted by church ministers – most from the Church of England – but the picture is changing rapidly. Since 2000, the Church of England has kept central records of services carried out by its parish clergy, and it is possible to use these records to build up a picture of the current situation. In 2000, 46 per cent of funerals were led by Church of England parish clergy, either in the church first followed by crematorium or cemetery, or exclusively at the crematorium or cemetery. By 2009, this had dwindled to 38 per cent, with a general pattern of a 1 per cent decrease per annum. If current trends continue, it will not take long for this figure to be down to 25 per cent.

This is not the whole story. Funerals are also conducted by retired clergy for whom records are not kept, and, indeed, by hospital and hospice chaplains who have formed a pastoral relationship with the deceased and their family prior to the death. The Co-op's research for 2009 suggested that two-thirds of funerals were still conducted by religious ministers or officials. If we estimate that 10 per cent of those were by religious leaders of other faiths and other Christian denominations, this suggests that about 56 per cent of funerals are conducted by the Church of England. This is a big decrease from the 70 per cent estimate at the time of the 1998 debate. The trend is unmistakable. Given that most civil celebrants provide an excellent service which accords well with what families want for the funeral, it is to be expected that the numbers of services they conduct will increase.

There has been a tendency amongst clergy to assume that it is their right to conduct funerals. One of the most common complaints from clergy concerning funerals is how often they are arranged with the crematorium without checking with them first as to whether they are available. However, the funeral director faces a dilemma. It is likely that he or she will try to make the arrangement while the bereaved family is still with them: the family are vulnerable and the funeral director will want to ensure that they are not left with uncertainties for longer than is possible. If the minister is out and does not return the call quickly, the family is left in a difficult position. Particularly where they do not have any strong religious affiliation, to know that a civil celebrant could do an equally good job and is prepared to indicate availability provides peace of mind in a time of grief and anxiety.

This raises a wider point about the relationship of church ministers and undertakers. If the Church takes seriously its ministry at the time of death, then we need to work hard to build good relationships with funeral directors. On arriving in a new town, the funeral director should certainly be a port of call for a new minister. Provision of a mobile phone number in addition to a landline will ensure that the funeral director can contact the minister when necessary. In some areas, local clergy are exploring the possibility of providing a 'duty minister' rota, so that a clergyperson will always be available for funerals, whenever they are arranged. This may be at odds with the Church of England's understanding of parishes, but it does fit into an understanding of chaplaincy ministry which is based, not on geographical location, but on links with a particular community. It could easily be seen that the bereaved community have particular needs which could be met by a chaplaincy service.

The changes that have taken place in funerals over the last 20 years in location, content and those conducting the service should lead us to ask the fundamental question: 'Who is the funeral for?' If we are clear about that, and what its purpose should be, it may then be easier to consider what should go into it.

Who is the funeral for?

This may seem like an odd question because a funeral is surely about the person who has died. But is it for that person, or is it for the people who are left behind? It is not necessarily helpful to see these two questions as being in opposition to each other: a funeral should be for both the living and the dead. However, the problem we have encountered in many funerals today is that they are seen as either/or questions – either the funeral is for the living, or it is for the dead.

1. The funeral is for the person who has died

There is an important moment in the service, called the commendation, which generally happens towards the end of the service when the minister commends the person who has died to the mercy of God. In the modern service of the Church of England, the prayer that is normally said at this point goes as follows:

> God our creator and redeemer,
> by your power Christ conquered death
> and entered into glory.

> Confident of his victory
> and claiming his promises
> we entrust N to your mercy,
> in the name of Jesus our Lord,
> who died and is alive
> and reigns with you,
> now and forever.
> **Amen**

What is being said in this prayer is that the person who has died is being entrusted to God at that moment; it does not merely acknowledge that the dead person is already in the arms of God. This may be problematic for many Christians who believe that once a person is dead, there is nothing that can be done to affect whether or not they are welcomed by God. Either they made a decision in life to accept Christ's death for them on the cross – in which case, they will know the mercy and grace of God as soon as death comes – or they did not accept Christ in life, in which case a prayer by a minister at the funeral can make no difference.

In Chapter 2, I will consider in much more detail the theological assumptions behind these statements. At this stage, it is just worth observing that a funeral as a rite of passage can be said to bring something about in a ritual way that has already happened in an actual way. Let us consider the parallel of the baptism of an adult believer. When an adult is baptised, he or she goes down into the water to be baptised and emerges as a new person. The symbolism speaks of the drowning of the old person in the waters of death in order that they might rise again with Christ in his new life. At a literal level, it is possible to say that the person was 'born again' when they accepted Christ; but their baptism acknowledges in a ritual way what actually happened when the person baptised made the decision for Christ.

So it is the same at a funeral. It may well be that at the moment of death, the person actually knows grace and the mercy of God in a real way that cannot be known in life, but the ritual knowing of that comes about at the commendation in the funeral service.

This has a very significant effect on a practice that is becoming increasingly common in this country. There is often a brief act of committal at the crematorium or cemetery, which very few attend, followed by a much larger service in the church, which is inevitably billed as a thanksgiving service. At this thanksgiving service, there is no coffin because the body has already been committed for burial or cremation. Somehow it seems as though the underlying psychology behind this is that people will be upset by or sad at its sight, and at a thanksgiving the mood should be more upbeat. This practice is far more common in the USA, but it is becoming much more common in this country too, both amongst people of committed faith and those with little or no lived-out faith.

But if there is a parallel with baptism, it seems odd that in this case the person at the heart of the ritual is excluded from it. Some people would say that the dead cannot know or mind whether they are there or not, and that if it is about a spiritual journey the person makes, then having the body present makes no difference. Thomas Long is an American writer who dislikes this practice: he suggests that having a funeral without a body present is like having a wedding without a bride, or Holy Communion without using the actual elements of bread and wine.[8] Christianity is not a faith which deals with only 'spiritual' things: we have the sacraments as actual physical things to remind us of our actual physical bodies and the actual physical reality of the world that God created and declared to be good. To have the actual physical body at the funeral reminds us all of that.

This also means that we need to be careful about what we say about the body. It is too easy to declare that it is merely a shell and that the person is not there. But at the heart of our faith is the resurrection of the body, not merely the transmigration of our souls, so we need to deal with the body that we have in this life with a little respect. Thomas Lynch is an undertaker and a poet, based in Michigan, USA. He recounts the story of a Christian minister in his home town who tried to comfort the mother of a teenage girl who had died of leukaemia by saying to her, 'It's OK, that's not her – it's just a shell.' He was rewarded with a swift slap from the woman who replied, 'I'll tell you when *it's* 'just a shell . . . for now and until I tell you otherwise, *she's* my daughter'.[9]

Our bodies matter in our faith, and by excluding them from their own funerals, we undermine their importance. The Christian pilgrimage or journey begins at our baptism – whether that is as a baby in a font or as a believer in a baptistery pool – and ends at our funeral. Surely we should mark that ending as we marked the beginning, by being present in our coffins before the altar of God?

2. The funeral is for the family and mourners

One of the triggers for the Reformation in Europe in the sixteenth century was the unease that the Reformers felt at the way that the dead and dying were treated in medieval Roman Catholic theology. It was possible to buy indulgences from the Church whilst you were alive

---

8. See his book *Accompany them with Singing: The Christian Funeral*, Louisville: Westminster John Knox Press, 2009, for an excellent defence of ensuring that the body is present at the funeral and for good common sense throughout.
9. Thomas Lynch, *The Undertaking Life: Studies from the Dismal Trade*, London: Vintage, 1998, p.23.

which would assist you when you died to get to heaven with God. It was also important to receive the Last Rites before you died, and there was no question that the funeral was for the person who had died as much as for the living who were left behind.

Part of the Protestants' reaction to this was to insist that the funeral was not for the dead, but for the living. In the order for the Burial of the Dead from the Church of England 1662 *Book of Common Prayer*, for example, there is no commendation at all, merely an acknowledgement that God has already taken 'unto himself the soul of our dear brother here departed'. The Puritans were quite clear that the funeral had no impact on the dead person at all and could probably be avoided. Writing in 1634, a Puritan in New England, named John Canne, suggested that the best thing was to bury the dead completely without prayers, sermon, or any ceremony whatsoever.

While most people can see the benefit of having a funeral ceremony, the sense that it is really for the living rather than the dead has persisted in many churches. It is not simply a question of whether or not the body of the person should be present at the service; even where they are, the main purpose of the service is to comfort the family and to remind them of their eternal destiny. When I was training to be ordained, one of the most influential books on the 'occasional offices' – baptisms, marriages and funerals – was entitled *Brief Encounters*. Written in 1985 by Wesley Carr, a former Dean of Westminster Abbey, it has had a profound effect on ministers in the Church of England for nearly 30 years. Carr argues that the funeral is not for the dead, but for the bereaved:

> The funeral is for the bereaved, not for the corpse. The minister is not dismissing a soul from this world, nor is he merely disposing of mortal remains ... The funeral, therefore is for those who are left.[10]

But I think Dean Carr is wrong – a funeral is for the dead person as well, not just for those left behind. I think it is unhelpful to speak of 'the corpse', because in the coffin is a person who is commended to God. They are beloved of those who have gathered to mourn and they are beloved of God; they are not simply an object to be thrown into the ground or onto the fire.

I am aware that this can lead to a difficult thought: it is not simply a shell that is going into the fire or the ground – it is a person. It feels very different to say that we are burying a person rather than a corpse! Families will sometimes say that nobody needs to go on to the crematorium after a church service for the committal because it is only

---

10. Wesley Carr, *Brief Encounters: Pastoral Ministry through the Occasional Offices*, London: SPCK, 1985, p.108.

about the disposal of an inanimate object. Indeed, there are clergy who agree with this view and do not go either. I am extremely uncomfortable about this and believe strongly that it is part of my role to be there, even when the family is not there to accompany the deceased on the final part of their journey. I am comforted by the fact that good funeral directors will do similarly, and many will insist on some minimal ritual at the crematorium which they will conduct themselves if there is no one else to do it.

One way in which we can mark the fact that there is a person still at the centre of the service is to be part of the movement of the funeral with the coffin at its heart. It is to be welcomed that family members are still often involved in carrying the coffin into the church. It is not an easy thing to do – it is much easier to hand it over to professionals who are used to the task. However, often the deceased will have carried the very people who now carry them when they were small, and they now return the favour. At the end of a church service, I have often encouraged the whole congregation to walk with the coffin as far as the hearse. It is not far, and the walking is more symbolic than actual, but it accompanies the person who has died on the final stage of their journey.

Some people reading this will be profoundly uncomfortable, thinking that I speak of the person who has died as though they are still with us. In the West over the last few centuries we have encouraged a complete separation from the living and the dead, and we are not encouraged to say that the dead have any part with us. We rightly say that we should not try and communicate with the spirits of the dead – certainly the Bible gives examples of the perils of doing this – and the pastoral experience of those who have had to counsel people who have become involved in this would point to many dangers.

However, this does not mean that we cannot recognise the community of the dead alongside us, though in another realm. The ancient Church Father, Hippolytus, in the third century, spoke of the Church as being an ark on a stormy sea. On that sea are communities of both the living and the dead, and the ship is heading for the kingdom of God. It is only when God's kingdom comes in fullness that we reach our destination. It is not that the dead have arrived there, or that they have reached a full stop; simply that they have changed the manner of their living till they get there. This acknowledgement of the presence of the dead may feel uncomfortable to us, and yet the bereaved will often say that they sense the presence of their loved one with them. Perhaps we need not fear this: when we say in the Creeds that we believe in the Communion of Saints, we are acknowledging their ongoing life in another place.

Other cultures are much more relaxed about this. In many traditional cultures, the role of ancestors is very important in cultural thinking: the ancestors are still amongst the living, not banished to a place beyond heart and mind. In Mexico, there is a festival each year called The Day of the Dead, which falls around All Souls' Tide on 2 November when families go to cemeteries for picnics and include their loved one in their picnic. Stories are told of the one who has died, and there is a general acknowledgement of their presence, apart and yet amongst them.

What is the funeral for?

If we have established that the funeral is for the dead *and* for the living, we can also ask the question, what is the funeral for? A number of answers can be given. In 1965, the Church of England set up a Liturgical Commission to look at funeral rites. In response to this question, the Commission came up with five primary answers:

- To secure the reverent disposal of the corpse
- To commend the deceased to the care of our heavenly Father
- To proclaim the glory of our risen life in Christ here and hereafter
- To remind us of the awful certainty of our own coming death and judgement
- To make plain the eternal unity of Christian people, living and departed, in the risen and ascended Christ.[11]

Looking at this list, it can be seen that some of these purposes are for the benefit of the deceased – securing the reverent disposal of the corpse and commending him or her to God. Others focus on the living – proclaiming our risen life in Christ and reminding us of death and judgement. The last point is an important reminder of the Communion of Saints – what the old Church of England *Book of Common Prayer* describes as the Church militant – the living – and the Church triumphant – the departed.

The third point above is, of course, central to a Christian understanding of funerals and it gives meaning and hope in the midst of despair: we proclaim the glory of our risen life in Christ here and hereafter. However, it is a point that could easily be lost in many funerals today. What is looked for in modern funerals is thanksgiving for the life that has gone. As people find it increasingly hard to believe in any form of resurrection life beyond death, it is an important task of the Church to ensure that we continue to proclaim its truth in the midst of death. The notes to the modern Church of England service make

---

11. *Alternative Services, Second Series*, London: Church of England Liturgical Commission, 1965, p.105-6.

clear that a sermon should be preached which proclaims the gospel in the context of the death of this particular person. At the heart of the gospel is the fact that, because Jesus died and rose again, death is not simply an end but a new beginning.

In this list, there is very little about the life of the deceased being important. The bereaved are to be comforted by being reminded of the Christian hope, not by being reminded of the life of the person who has died. In fact, it was only with this revision of the funeral service in 1965 that there was even space within the liturgy of the Church of England to call the deceased by name. Until that time, you could get through the service without ever having to name them. Small wonder that some clergy forgot what the person's name was if they had grown used to ministering in an era when that information was not important!

It seems to me that there are two notable omissions from the 1965 list of purposes of the funeral:

1. To give thanks

Many funerals nowadays in this country are described as 'services of thanksgiving' rather than funerals, and often mourners are told that the most important thing is to give thanks for the life of the person who has died. When the Church of England brought out a new service in 2000 for funerals, it provided an introduction in which the minister declared what the purposes of the funeral was:

> We have come here today
> to remember before God our *brother/sister N*,
> to give thanks for *his/her* life;
> to commend *him/her* to God our merciful redeemer and judge;
> to commit *his/her* body to be buried / cremated,
> and to comfort one another in our grief.

The first two purposes from 1965 are retained, but now there is much more focus on the person who has died. We remember the person and we give thanks. That is why tributes from family and friends can be such helpful additions to the funeral, because they remind us of the reasons why we can give thanks. I am aware that some ministers are concerned that personal tributes can hijack a service – they can often be very long and, if the person is not used to public speaking, they can be poorly delivered. But the very inclusion of the tribute speaks of the person and the reasons why everyone is gathered there. Even when there are difficulties created as a result of a tribute, there are very often still good reasons to include them.

When there is no one amongst the family or friends who is able to give a tribute, it is important that the minister takes the time to speak about the person who has died. This is not an easy task, especially when the minister has never met the person, but it is a vital skill to master in leading funeral services today. If we take seriously the fact that a funeral should offer the opportunity to give thanks for a life, then it is only reasonable that we speak about that life during the service.

2. To mourn

It seems odd to say that there is no mention of the need to mourn in the service, and yet it is true. The 1965 Liturgical Commission wondered whether to include 'the consolation of the mourners', but felt that it came through in all the other points mentioned. Similarly, we have noted that one of the aims of the modern Church of England service is 'to comfort one another in our grief'. However, there is a difference between comforting those who mourn and actually mourning; surely, one of the purposes of the funeral should actually be to mourn, not just to comfort those who do. Why is this omitted?

In St Paul's first letter to the Thessalonians – and this may well be the earliest letter that we have in the New Testament that was written by Paul – he is facing the anguish of Christians in Thessalonica who have seen members of their community die. It was anticipated that no Christian would die before Jesus came again – Jesus' own resurrection would be followed very swiftly by the general resurrection of all believers. So Paul has to explain how it is that some Christians are beginning to die. In setting out his answer, he says, 'we do not want you to be uninformed, brothers and sisters, about those who have died, so that you may not grieve as others do who have no hope' (1 Thessalonians 4:13).

Paul does not say that he did not want the believers to grieve – he says that they should not do so *without hope*. However, it does feel today as though Christians are told that we should not grieve. This goes along with an attitude – which is as prevalent among people of no faith as it is among those with a very committed faith – that grief has no place in a funeral service and that it should focus only on thanksgiving.

Paul Sheppy describes a Christian funeral as 'a remembrance of this person's life in the context of the Easter event';[12] in other words, we make sense of our own deaths by looking at Jesus' death and resurrection. Both aspects are vital in making sense of a funeral. Easter is not just one day; it is three. Before we can make sense of the joy that Easter brings, we must also understand the sorrow and desolation that came with Good Friday and Holy Saturday. Imagine the sorrow that the Blessed Virgin Mary, the disciples, Mary Magdalene and Jesus'

---

12. Sheppy, *Death Liturgy and Ritual, Vol 1*, p.8.

other friends felt at his death. This is hard for us to do because we know the end of the story. However, they did not, and so they felt real sorrow.

We are often reminded today of the importance of grief; we should let our feelings show and not try and suppress them. In its pastoral care, the Church has been keen to use the insights from modern counselling methods and psychology and apply them to grief management. It is strange, then, that when it comes to the main ritual surrounding death, there is no explicit acknowledgement of the place of grief within the service.

One of the reasons why this goes unchallenged is because our society does not want to be reminded of the need to grieve. Funeral services are often deliberately designed as thanksgiving services: mourners are asked not to wear black and are often instructed to wear bright colours to reflect the deceased's personality.[13] Popular readings remind the mourners that 'death is nothing at all' and that there is no need to stand at the grave and weep because the deceased 'is not there: [he] did not die'.[14] If we take these words literally, why would there be any need to be sad?

But a funeral is not a trivial event. We are marking the death of a loved one, not the extraction of a tooth. As we will see in the next chapter, Scripture has a robust attitude to death and recognises it as awful. Why are we so frightened to do likewise? Our society talks today about people 'passing' or being 'gone'; it finds it almost impossible to say that they have died, so uses euphemisms instead.

The modern funeral service has improved enormously over the last 50 years in focusing on the person who has died. We need not think of this as a non-Christian development: we follow a Saviour who lived an earthly life and the Gospels are full of incidents from his life. To recognise the significance of each of our lives is entirely in keeping with this. But let us not pretend that death does not cause us grief and that our funerals should simply be times to offer thanksgiving. The Liverpudlian poet, Roger McGough – no doubt with his tongue firmly in his cheek – expresses an important truth:

I don't want any of that
'We're gathered here today
to celebrate his life, not mourn his passing.'
Oh yes you are. Get one thing straight,
you're not here to celebrate,
but to mourn till it hurts.

---

13. I have even officiated at a funeral where mourners were asked to wear something in leopard print in honour of the deceased who clearly enjoyed a wild sense of fashion!
14. Taken from two of the most popular readings at funerals – 'Death is nothing at all' by Canon Henry Scott Holland and 'Do not stand at my grave and weep' by Mary Elizabeth Fry – see chapters 2 and 3 for further details of these readings.

> I want wailing and gnashing of teeth.
> I want sobs, and I want them uncontrollable,
> I want women flinging themselves on the coffin,
> and I want them inconsolable.
>
> Don't dwell upon my past but on your future,
> for what you see is what you'll be,
> and sooner than you think.
> So get weeping. Fill yourselves with dread.
> For I am not sleeping. I am dead.[15]

I would much prefer to preach a sermon at a funeral service after this, offering people hope in the midst of 'what you see is what you'll be', than after readings telling people that death is nothing and suggesting that there is no reason to mourn.

The sad thing about Christian funerals is that we have wonderful resources in Scripture that enable us to say the sad things whilst still holding on to hope in God, but we do not use them. The Psalms are full of examples of the psalmist pouring out his (or maybe her) heart to God: he complains that, 'I am weary with my crying; my throat is parched. My eyes grow dim with waiting for my God' (Psalm 69:3). This seems to be a state of being that those who grieve would identify with, so why do we not provide space for such sentiments within our funeral services?

Funerals in Britain today have become focused on celebration and thanksgiving. This is true whether they are conducted by a Christian minister or a civil celebrant. As Christians, we have reasons to give thanks for the life past, and we have hope in the future. However, because of that hope, we should also be able to mourn. I suspect that it is much more difficult to allow for mourning and grief in a non-religious ceremony because there is no meaning to it and it can only turn to despair. I think one of the greatest gifts we can offer our society at the time of death is to allow people to mourn at funerals and provide meaning and hope in the midst of it.

In this book, I consider each aspect of the funeral service – the readings, the prayers, the music – and offer examples in the substantive part of the book as well as the second resources section of what can be used. Their usefulness should be considered within the parameters of this chapter:

- What significance do they have for the dead – either in calling the person to mind or in sending them on their way to God?
- Do they help the bereaved come to terms with a loved one's death?
- Do they give expression to the grief felt at a funeral?
- Do they provide hope for the future?

---

15. Roger McGough, 'I am not sleeping' from *Selected Poems*, London: Penguin, 2006.

A funeral is for the dead as well as the living, and the resources used, as well as the structure of the service, should allow both needs to be met. Scripture and the Christian tradition are full of resources that answer these questions. What we have discovered in recent times is that there are many other resources that can also be called upon. As Christians, we can embrace the latter whilst still holding on to the importance of Scripture and tradition.

Before we look at these resources, we should consider death itself and how we understand it as Christians, and the impact that Christ's death has had upon it.

Two
Whatever happened to death?

In May 1910, after the death of King Edward VII, one of the canons at St Paul's Cathedral, Henry Scott Holland, preached a sermon. He entitled it 'The King of Terrors' and included some words which have since become very famous:

> Death is nothing at all. It does not count. I have only slipped away into the next room. Nothing has happened. Everything remains exactly as it was. I am I, and you are you, and the old life that we lived so fondly together is untouched, unchanged. Whatever we were to each other, that we are still. Call me by the old familiar name. Speak of me in the easy way which you always used. Put no difference into your tone. Wear no forced air of solemnity or sorrow. Laugh as we always laughed at the little jokes that we enjoyed together. Play, smile, think of me, pray for me. Let my name be ever the household word that it always was. Let it be spoken without an effort, without the ghost of a shadow upon it. Life means all that it ever meant. It is the same as it ever was. There is absolute and unbroken continuity. What is this death but a negligible accident? Why should I be out of mind because I am out of sight? I am but waiting for you, for an interval, somewhere very near, just round the corner. All is well. Nothing is hurt; nothing is lost. One brief moment and all will be as it was before. How we shall laugh at the trouble of parting when we meet again![16]

Poor Henry Scott Holland! This piece remains a very popular reading at funerals and seems to offer comfort to those who mourn. Indeed, in the previous chapter, we saw how in many parts of the world – and indeed in the West in the past – to say that the dead are in a different room is not such a strange thought. Just because someone has died does not mean that there cannot be unbroken communion with them. However, this is not what Scott Holland meant in his sermon. He was contrasting two opposing views of death, of which this was one. Just as important is the view that death is an awful tragedy and worthy of deep grief. Scott Holland's point in the sermon was that it is only in the death of Christ that we are able to bring both these views together.

What we need to do is to see what the Bible tells us about death; there is not simply one straightforward message. Think of the anguish that Jesus felt in the Garden of Gethsemane as he faced his own death;

---

16. This sermon is now out of copyright as Canon Scott Holland died in 1918, so it is possible to read a full transcript online. I have copied it from http://en.wikisource.org/wiki/The_King_of_Terrors (accessed 17 April 2013).

he certainly wasn't thinking 'death is nothing at all' at that moment! Similarly, in Acts 9 we are told the story of an early Christian believer, Dorcas (or Tabitha) who died. The response of her friends and widows was to weep at her death (9:39), even though this took place after Jesus had risen from the dead, so there was an understanding that as Christians we have the hope of resurrection.

One of the most difficult dilemmas that Christian ministers face in conducting funerals is that they know very little about the faith of the person who has died. Although about two-thirds of the funerals in this country are still conducted by a Christian minister – though this figure is declining – most of these will not be for committed churchgoers or for those with an active faith. Should we be mentioning the hope of resurrection to the families of those who did not appear to show any faith in Jesus in their own lives? This is a very difficult issue, but it is important in a book of funerals that we at least consider this subject and outline some of the views held!

Three views of death in the Bible

In his sermon, Henry Scott Holland tried to distinguish between two different attitudes to death. I have built on these categories, looking at what the Bible says. I have also used the insights from the American preacher Thomas G. Long, who provides some very helpful thoughts in his book, *Accompany them with Singing*.[17]

1. The final enemy Death

Throughout most of the Old Testament, there was no widely held belief in resurrection: when you were dead, you were dead. Indeed, the place of death, which was known as Sheol, was seen as a place where God was absent. We see this attitude expressed in many of the psalms. The psalmist is clear that the dead cannot praise God (see, for example, Psalm 88:10 or 115:17. Even by the time of Jesus, the religious group of Jews known as the Sadducees mocked Jesus about the resurrection: they did not believe in it because there is no mention of resurrection in the first five books of the Bible, the Pentateuch.

This attitude underlines the first view of death that comes through in the Bible, which is that it is awful and to be seen as the enemy Death. It came into the world as a result of the Fall and was not part of God's original intentions for his creation: in that sense, it is not natural and is part of the disorder of the world. St Paul describes death as the last enemy to be destroyed (1 Corinthians 15:26), and whilst he is clear that its destruction is inevitable because of the death and resurrection of Christ, he recognises its presence as still a force for evil in the world.

---

17. Thomas G. Long, *Accompany them with Singing*, Louisville: Westminster John Knox Press, 2009.

In some ways, Death is representative of all that is still wrong with our world. We speak of this life as being 'a Vale of Tears' – because of illness and suffering as much as death; because of natural disasters which sweep the world and cause havoc; because of injustice and what Robert Burns first described as 'man's inhumanity to man'.

I am aware that if we take too literal an interpretation of Scripture's message that death is a result of the Fall, we have a problem. If there had been no Fall, does this mean that nobody would ever have died? If that is the case, how would we have found room for them all on Earth? I think this emphasises the problems that result from an over-literal interpretation of Scripture. Perhaps the answer to the question would be that human beings would not have continued to populate the earth for so many thousands of years, but that seems equally unsatisfactory. It seems to me that we should accept the biblical witness as a symbolic worldview without trying to press the worldview into actual facts of historical events.

Of course, there are occasions when we reach a person's funeral with a measure of relief that they are now free from suffering, or with thanksgiving for a long life well lived, but that does not mean that we should ignore the biblical witness towards death, which sees it as unnatural and to be considered as part of the brokenness of creation. As Christians, we look forward to the time that St John saw in Revelation 21, when there will be a new heaven and a new earth, where 'death will be no more; mourning and crying and pain will be no more' (Revelation 21:4). But in the meantime, we still live with those things, and so we mourn.

The right Christian response to this enemy Death is to lament, which at its heart is a complaint against God for what has happened. I will consider further in Chapter 3 resources that we have to do this and what the Bible teaches us about lament. Sometimes, perhaps particularly at the funerals of Christians who died with a strong faith after a long life, we feel that we should not mourn at all. But what we are doing is not just mourning the loss of that particular person; we are also mourning the brokenness of our world in which death still continues.

2. The individual death

I have deliberately described death here with a lower-case 'd' rather than with the capital of Death, the final enemy. Here we are simply acknowledging the fact that everyone will die. Sometimes this can feel desperate. Anyone who has been at a funeral of a baby or a young child will know the feeling of overwhelming sorrow that is in the church or chapel as we say goodbye to a life cut off prematurely. Indeed, there are particular issues that arise when leading a funeral of a child, which will be dealt with in Chapter 8. Whilst the sorrow is particularly acute on those occasions, we feel sad whenever death is met unexpectedly. Even when someone has prepared well for death and lived a good life, the sense of sorrow is still understandably strong. Someone whom we loved dearly has died, and we will not see them again in this life: it is a justifiable reason to mourn.

However, there can be occasions when the sorrow of loss mingles with the acknowledgement of thanksgiving. It is this that Scott Holland was talking about in that part of his sermon that is so often quoted. Nowadays we say that the best death is when a person dies suddenly and without ostensible pain, perhaps when they are asleep and at peace with the world. Here there is a feeling that this was a good death, for which we give thanks.

It is a fairly modern attitude that considers this a good death. In former times, a death was good if it was well prepared for, if the person was aware that it was coming and had the chance to say goodbye to family and friends – even if they had to endure pain through that time. Personally, I think this sort of death still has many advantages – particularly now that pain control in the West can be so expertly managed by palliative doctors and nurses and through the care that hospices give.

Thomas Lynch says that in his town in northern USA, about eight people will die each year for every 1000 head of population. However, there is one statistic – which he describes as 'THE BIG ONE' – which is unavoidable: in his town, as in every town and community, there is a 100 per cent death rate.[18] None of us can avoid it! Most of us go through life trying to ignore the fact, and hope that we will not have to face death for many years. The French writer, François de la Rochefoucauld, commented wryly that 'death, like the sun, is not to be looked at steadily'.[19] However, Tony Walter has observed that 'the wise person lives in its light'.[20] By living in the light of the fact of death, we find the opportunity to gain wisdom, and we are reassured that we will not all go on living in our mortal bodies for ever, becoming frailer and more and more subject to the indignities and illnesses of old age.

Of course, this is something that some people find frightening. The extreme response to this is cryogenics, by which a person is frozen in the moments after death in the hope that they can be revived once the secret to immortality is found. Most of us would not go this far. However, it does feel as though some people who submit themselves repeatedly to the plastic surgeon's knife are living just as much in a state of denial about old age and death as those who want to live for ever in this life.

---

18. Thomas Lynch, *The Undertaking Life: Studies from the Dismal Trade*, London: Vintage, 1998, p.5.
19. François de la Rochefoucauld, *Maxims* (1678) No. 26.
20. Tony Walter, *The Revival of Death*, London: Routledge, 1994.

When someone reaches death, having lived in the light of its inevitability, there can be a strong sense of thanksgiving at their funeral. Alongside the sorrow at losing a loved friend or family member, it is not surprising that there are occasions when the overwhelming sense at some funerals is one of thanksgiving. In these circumstances, it seems entirely fitting to describe a funeral as a 'service of thanksgiving'. Personally, I prefer not to call such services 'celebrations', though I am aware that they are often called this. Death does not seem to be something to celebrate, whilst thanksgiving is directed beyond ourselves to God, to give thanks for a person's life.

3. Death in Christ

Thomas Long reminds us that there is a third category that the Bible speaks of about death, and that is a spiritual death that takes place in our lifetimes. St Paul says in Romans 6:4 and Colossians 2:12 that we were buried with Christ in our baptisms: in other words, at the very start of our Christian pilgrimage, we die symbolically to our old lives and rise again with Christ to a new life. This is what Jesus was talking about when he encountered Nicodemus in John 3. He said that if anyone wanted to see the kingdom of God, they must be born again, or born from above: in other words, it is as though the person must die the first time and then be reborn in the waters of baptism.

It is a theme that Jesus comes back to often in the Gospels, when he says that if anyone wants to be a true follower of him, they must take up their cross. This is a theme that recurs in each of the Synoptic Gospels: in Matthew 16:24-6, Mark 8:34-7, Luke 9:23-6. The power of Jesus' words has become somewhat diluted in the English language: we talk of 'everyone having a cross to bear', meaning that we need to put up with particular hardships or inconveniences. But when Jesus said these words, he, and all his listeners, could only have been put in mind of death. The only reason anybody carried a cross was to end up dead on it.

So death should not be a subject that is hidden from the average Christian, and yet we still find it difficult to deal with. There is something strange about taking babies for baptism and speaking immediately of a rite that is full of the language of drowning and death. I sometimes wonder whether parents would be so keen to allow me to hold their baby if they fully understood the theology behind it!

Similarly, themes of death are very important in the other sacrament of faith which we receive from the Gospels – the Eucharist or Holy Communion or Mass. Sadly, this service has often been the source of division rather than unity amongst Christians, because our understanding of what is happening whilst it is taking place differs. However, whether we believe that the bread and wine have mysteriously become the body and blood of Christ, whether we think the service is just a memorial act, or whether we hold any other theological interpretation somewhere between these two points, we are all agreed that the central event we remember is the death of Christ.

In other words, from the day that we are baptised, when we are said to go down into the waters of death with Jesus, we live our Christian pilgrimage sustained by the Eucharist, which puts us again in mind of Jesus' death. We are also reminded of his words to take up our own cross, that we might put to death our selfish desires and all that is within us that does not lead us towards God. By the time we reach our funerals, notions of death should not be new to us!

Douglas Davies, Professor at the Centre for Life and Death Studies at Durham University, carried out some very interesting research in the late 1980s about the recognition of the dead in the Eucharist. He interviewed a number of churchgoers of different ages. Half of adults aged under the age of 34 and 47 per cent of those aged over 65 said that they sensed the presence of a loved one at the Eucharist – not simply that they were reminded of them, but that they actually felt their presence. This fits well with the understanding of the living and the dead being alongside one another that we looked at in Chapter 1.

It should also mean that when we come to the funeral of a Christian friend or family member, we should see the service in the wider context of Christian worship. In the days of the early Church this was much more marked. A Communion wafer or host was often placed on the tongue of the deceased as a *viaticum*, a sign of spiritual sustenance to take them to the place of God; the Peace would be shared amongst the mourners; Communion would be distributed around the graveside; and mourners wore white robes as a reminder of the deceased's baptism. Sadly, we have lost most of these points of reference at a funeral; perhaps we should look to regain them.

What happens to those who die?

By focusing on the notion of death in Christ, we are reminded of a particularly obvious problem that faces many Christian ministers when they are asked to conduct a funeral. On many occasions, we are asked to take a funeral where the person who has died had no expressed faith in their lives and were not part of a Christian community. It may be that they were baptised, but, certainly as far as the Church of England is concerned, it is not a requirement that someone is baptised for them to be buried by a Christian minister (or, indeed, contrary to much popular opinion, for them to be able to get married in church). It is all very well to speak of dying to sin at our baptism and rising to new life, but should we speak of the hope of heaven to those who lived lives denying its existence? The two extreme views can be seen in the following two statements from vicars about the approach they take. Both quotations are real examples of responses I have heard on this subject:

> When the deceased or their family are Christians, I preach about heaven. Otherwise, I preach about hell.

> When I preach from John 14:6, I only ever say the first part of the verse, 'I am the way, and the truth, and the life'. I never add the bit after that says, 'No one comes to the Father except through me.'

The first quotation encapsulates an understanding of Christian faith in which it is clear who is going to heaven and who is going to hell, and that it is important to make a decision either way. The second view refuses to accept that there might be something distinctive about Jesus' ministry which provides unique access to God.

I think the first thing that we must always do when we speak on this subject is to acknowledge the limits of our understanding. This is why the first statement above is difficult for me: it presumes a knowledge about people's hearts that none of us have. These are ultimately matters of faith: however strong our belief is, we must ultimately let God be God. When I was at theological college, there were some who were very concerned to say that penal substitution was the only acceptable understanding of the atonement and others who insisted that we must see representation as the truth, or expiation. Whilst I accept that it is important to take seriously what Scripture tells us about the meaning of Christ's death, it paints a diverse picture. By insisting that our understanding is the right one, we often deny that diversity and refuse to come to the matter in humility and accepting that we may be wrong. Furthermore, God may teach us more about himself and his relationship with unlikely people in the lives of those whom we dismiss as having no relationship with him than in the lives of some faithful church members.

This is a matter of discussion in which Christians disagree strongly, but here are some of the views that are held and, I hope, a way in which we can offer hope within funeral ministry with integrity.

1. Jesus only died for those who were going to believe in him

The most extreme form of this view is seen in the doctrine of predestination and double predestination. This holds that God knew from the beginning of time who was going to believe in him, and it was predestined that they would be saved whilst others would not.

The logical inference from this leads to double predestination, which says that not only did God know who was going to be saved, but he also knew who was going to be damned and, in its extreme form, holds that Jesus only died for those who were going to be saved.

It is possible to see the logic of this: why should Jesus die for those for whom it would make no difference and who would end up in hell anyway? However, few Christians would hold to this view. It has been officially condemned as heresy in Roman Catholic teaching, and important Reformed Protestant scholars such as Karl Barth have shown why it is not an acceptable understanding of God. It seems to go against the whole basis of Scripture in which God's love is poured out for his whole creation in generosity and love – 'God so loved the world', as John 3:16 reminds us, 'that he gave his only son'. To say that his Son only died for those who would ultimately believe suggests that others are beyond the limits of God's love.

2. Jesus died for everyone and we must accept his death for ourselves in order to gain the benefit

The most common way of understanding this is through the doctrine of penal substitution. This is based on the analogy of the law courts, whereby there was a penalty for sin that needed to be paid, just as there is a just punishment for a crime committed. Jesus paid the price for our sin. The analogy that is given is of a judge who decides that a criminal is guilty, and then comes down to the other side of the bench and pays the fine that is owing. At the heart of this thinking is that there is a price to pay, and that Jesus paid the price if we are prepared to accept that he did so on our behalf.

There are obviously limits to this analogy: it is unheard of for a judge to take such action, and many would not consider justice to be done in those circumstances. Furthermore, Jesus did a great deal more than pay a fine: he died for us.

To say that we must accept his death is only to acknowledge that people cannot be compelled into God's loving arms. Indeed, if everyone ultimately ends up saved by God, where is the place of judgement? There is an ethical problem with this. When people commit atrocities against us, we are reminded of Jesus' words to turn the other cheek and not to trade insults with insults. One of the reasons why we are able to do this is that we believe that God will ultimately judge us – and our aggressors – for our actions. If we think that God will simply accept those who do us wrong without there being any consequence for their wrongdoing, we may be less willing not to seek retaliation ourselves.

Of course, most of us do not encounter people who seem to commit really evil acts. Certainly, the funerals I conduct are not of bad people.

Furthermore, if a truly bad person were to repent and turn to Christ for forgiveness, they would not be punished in any event. Many people are also uncomfortable with the thought of the loving Father punishing his guiltless Son, describing this as 'cosmic child abuse'.

3. Jesus died for everyone and his death has eternal consequences for everyone

An alternative view to penal substitution is one of representation: that Jesus died as a representative of the whole of humanity. In his life, Jesus showed us what true humanity looked like: previously we had no model for that because the image of God in us had been spoilt through the Fall. Jesus, then, was a second Adam, showing us what we should be like. In his life, he is a representative human, and in his death, he dies a representative death. The most common way in which Jesus' death is described in the New Testament is as being 'on behalf of' humanity. Jesus' representative death did not result in the end of life for him: after death came resurrection, which means that our deaths are now transformed by resurrection too. Rather than seeing this in terms of a price to pay, this view suggests that there is a cost that must be paid, but once the cost has been satisfied, the work is done, whether or not people accept the cost.

This is not ultimately dependent upon human choices. Thomas Long draws a parallel with a cottager who lived in Normandy after the D-Day landings of June 1944. Whether or not he was liberated did not depend on him making a personal choice to be so. To suggest that personal choice is key for our salvation puts God's plan for creation at the mercy of human decision making.[21]

However, perhaps that is the point of God's love for us being so great that he gave us free will. Of course, in his power he could compel the salvation of all, but in his love, he allows us to choose whether or not to reject him. To impose compulsory heaven for all denies people the choice to say that they lived their lives without God and they do not want to live eternity with him.

Clearly, at a funeral, the minister cannot express the intricacies of Christian atonement theology. We must trust the mercy of God and offer hope to the families that, whether or not their loved one has chosen God, death need not be the end for anyone and that we all have the chance to choose life.

4. The choice of life after death

I want to offer one other view in addition to the choice between penal substitution where people are condemned to eternal punishment and a

---

21. Long, *Accompany them with Singing*, p.54.

representative view of the cross whereby we simply accept that all are saved. This is based on the writings of the twentieth-century Catholic theologian, Hans Urs von Balthasar (1905–1988).[22]

One of von Balthasar's chief concerns in his writing was to stress the importance of Holy Saturday in the three days of Easter. We all know that Jesus died on Good Friday and rose again on Easter Day, but the Saturday is often seen as an 'in-between' day in which nothing very significant happens. It is a day for the flower team to get the church looking its best for Easter Day, or perhaps even a day to conduct a wedding in the afternoon, but we do not think too much about its theological significance. It is a waiting day: Jesus is dead, but we know that that will not be the end of the story.

One of the difficulties we have is that the Bible tells us very little about this day. There is a reference in 1 Peter 3:18-19 to Jesus preaching to 'the spirits in prison' after he was put to death in the flesh, and in the following chapter we are told that 'the gospel was proclaimed even to the dead so that, though they had been judged in the flesh as everyone is judged, they might live in the spirit as God does' (4:6). There has been much discussion and dispute as to what these verses mean, but from them came the medieval notion of Jesus' Harrowing of Hell.

By this understanding, Jesus marched down to hell already victorious over death and rescued the spirits of the righteous among those who had already died. Von Balthasar was troubled by this because it meant that Jesus behaved in such a radically different way from the rest of us when he was dead. When we are dead we are absolutely incapable of doing anything, let alone marching triumphantly! He even thought the Apostles' Creed expressed it too strongly when it says that Jesus 'descended to the dead' because it ascribes an active verb – he descended – to one who was at that moment entirely passive. He preferred to speak of 'being with the dead'.

The pastoral implication that von Balthasar wanted to draw out is that Jesus was dead, just like we will all be dead one day. To suggest that he behaved differently in death from the rest of us is unhelpful. However, it is where this conclusion led him that has particular consequences in our funeral preaching. He rejected traditional Catholic teaching which said that Jesus did not go to the furthermost parts of hell: indeed, he did not accept that there are different chambers to hell, which medieval thinking had proposed.

The point that von Balthasar wished to make was that God reached down in Christ to the uttermost points of hell. This turns on its head the Old Testament thinking that God was not present in Sheol, the

---

22. What follows is a brief summary of his thinking, which is best expressed in his book *Mysterium Paschale: The Mystery of Easter*, San Francisco: Ignatius Press, 1990.

domain of the dead. Now the place of the dead is to be understood as hell, but it is a place where God himself has been in Christ. What makes this teaching so extraordinary is that von Balthasar's proposal that, even at the furthermost parts of hell, God's light is present, and that even at this point there is an opportunity to turn to God and know his light and his love.

This is at odds with most Protestant thinking which says that we must make a decision to follow Christ in this life: indeed, Jesus' parable of the Rich Man and Lazarus seems to support this Protestant viewpoint (Luke 16:19-31). However, von Balthasar's thinking could be seen to fit well with an understanding of 1 Peter 3 of Jesus rescuing the imprisoned spirits of the dead.

Von Balthasar is often accused of universalism here: one implication of his teaching could be that hell is empty. However, he maintains that even in hell we have the choice of whether or not to accept God: even at this point, we can choose to reject him, as we can in life.

Von Balthasar's teaching offers us a way of continuing to acknowledge the deceased and to pray for them at their funerals. If they die distant from the Church or not able to acknowledge the love of God in this life, the light of God can still reach them amongst the dead, because it has been there in Jesus on Holy Saturday.

This is a very difficult topic, because ultimately we cannot know what happens to us on death, and it must remain a matter of faith. It is rarely so straightforward as saying that Scripture offers one voice on the subject. This is why I think that humility and a trust in God's grace are the most important qualities that we should bring when we conduct funerals in these circumstances. I know that some readers will be very frustrated with me for not nailing my colours to the mast and indicating which view of atonement I hold to!

Ministers who carry out a large number of funerals for those with a strong faith and for those with very little expressed faith find it a huge privilege to share God's love at this critical time. I know also that it has offered opportunities for the families of those who have died to come into the regular life of the local congregation and grow stronger in their own faith. We should welcome these opportunities and use the funeral to offer hope and the possibility of grace for all.

Three
Comfort one another with these words

At the end of Chapter 1, I suggested that the resources that are used to make up the content of a funeral should be judged by the following criteria:

- What significance to they have for the dead – either in calling the person to mind or sending them on their way to God?
- Do they help the bereaved come to terms with their loved one's death?
- Do they give expression to the grief felt at a funeral?
- Do they provide hope for the future?

The next four chapters will look at these resources, which I think are made of three different types:

1. Words

Funerals are full of words. From the opening sentences that the minister reads as the coffin is brought into the church or chapel to the tributes paid by family members or friends, everyone expects a funeral to be made up of words. Perhaps that is why it is so startling – and often very liberating – to attend a funeral organised within the Quaker tradition. In those funerals, mourners are far more aware of the silence than of the speaking – and in the silence, they are given the opportunity to remember and mourn.

The next two chapters will consider the formal and informal words of a funeral, including passages from Scripture as well as poems that are often read at funerals today. It will also consider the place of the tribute and the sermon, and the prayers that are offered at various points in the service.

2. Music

Music has the power to evoke memories and emotions in a way that is often far more effective than the spoken word. People often remember singing a particular hymn at a funeral, and it may well be that that the hymn is forever thereafter associated with that occasion. Similarly, there may well be pieces of music that are always associated in people's minds with a loved one and they would like the opportunity to play the music as a tribute to that person. Chapter 5 considers the place of music at funerals in all their variety.

3. Symbols

From the releasing of a balloon at a graveside to the celebration of Holy Communion within the funeral service, symbols and symbolic actions suffuse the funeral service. The decision to bury a person or cremate them is not simply a decision about how to dispose of a body: it is an action full of symbolic meaning and says something – wittingly or unwittingly – about the belief held as to what happens to the body.

Some symbols, such as the celebration of Communion at a funeral service, go back to the earliest days of the Church, but they have been joined by modern practices, some of which can be individual to the deceased person. The emphasis in much funeral practice today is for each funeral to be a unique celebration of a unique life – we should not be surprised, then, that unique symbolic actions are brought in to accompany that life on its way from this life. Chapter 6 discusses these at greater length and their significance today.

But first, back to words: what do the words of the funeral service say about the life of the person who has died?

Words of Scripture

Although a common feature of most funerals today is a request for the reading of a poem or a favourite piece of prose, it is still likely that in any funeral conducted by a Christian minister, various passages of the Bible will be used at different points. I have mentioned the verses of Scripture that are often read as the coffin is brought in: there will probably also be a Bible reading at some other point in the service, and indeed, in more liturgical traditions such as the Church of England or the Roman Catholic Church, many of the set prayers through the service draw on words of Scripture for inspiration.

1. Opening sentences

> Jesus said to her, 'I am the resurrection and the life. Those who believe in me, even though they die, will live, and everyone who lives and believes in me will never die'. *John 11:25-26*

These have been the opening words of funeral services in England ever since the first English prayer book of 1549. They are still used in most Church of England services, and indeed in many other funeral rites at the beginning of the service. They proclaim confidently the hope that is at the heart of our faith: that those whose faith is founded on the death of Jesus and in his resurrection will not know eternal death, but will live with God for ever. If we consider the words in the light of the four purposes of funeral resources set out at the beginning of the chapter, they give voice to the fourth of these – offering hope for the future.

However, perhaps we should question whether they proclaim this hope too confidently at the beginning of the service. If the opening words of a service to mark the death of a loved one say that believers will live and never die, does that undermine the need to grieve that is part of a funeral service? These words undoubtedly comfort those who mourn, but they could also be read by some to deny the need to mourn, in a similar vein to Henry Scott Holland's words that 'death is nothing at all' and 'I have only slipped away into the next room.' If modern psychology has taught us that we need to be able to give expression to grief and not suppress it, it might be suggested that by opening a funeral service in this way, we are encouraging suppression rather than expression of grief.

I am not suggesting that these words of Jesus are not true and do not contain the very hope that we must proclaim at a Christian funeral to people filled with despair. I simply question whether placing them at the very start of a funeral service undermines another key purpose of a funeral, which is to give expression to grief felt at an awful loss.

Standard liturgies from various church traditions offer a number of succeeding verses to follow the opening words. The modern service authorised in the Church of England includes Paul's assertion from Romans 8 that nothing – not life, nor death, not things present or things to come, nothing in all creation – can separate us from God's love. Each verse is an assurance of God's love, a reminder of his promise to be with us, or a reminder of God's love for the whole world that he sent Jesus to die for us.

These are, of course, wonderful words of hope and faith. So why should we be uneasy about using them? My concern is that Scripture itself offers us a different response in the face of bleak suffering and despair. I will talk more about the response of the Psalms to human suffering and grief, but I think first it would be worth reflecting briefly on the death of Jesus and his use of Scripture.

The Gospel writers record seven different phrases that Jesus uttered whilst on the cross. Of these seven, Mark and Matthew only record one. Just before he died, Jesus cried out with a loud voice, 'My God, my God, why have you forsaken me?' They are words filled with despair and anguish – at that moment, the One who has been joined with God in the mystery of the Trinity from the beginning of time is now utterly cut off from him. In the very early Church, it is interesting to reflect that for the communities that only had access to Mark's and Matthew's Gospels – before the canon of Scripture had been put together –these are the only words they would have known from Jesus at the time of his death.

I suspect that these words resonate more with many bereaved people than Jesus' words of hope that those who believe will never die. When a loved one dies, it can feel as though we have lost a limb, and some people feel that they have been abandoned by God. Would it surprise them to know that Jesus himself also felt that searing despair?

What is even more significant about Jesus' words is that in crying out as he did, he was reciting the opening words of Psalm 22 – words that would have been used by Jews for generations in the synagogue and temple in their worship of God. When people came together to worship God, they did not simply accentuate the positive and focus on praise and hope. They also allowed themselves to express negative views about God. As we will explore below, what is so extraordinary about the Psalms is that they give voice to cries of anguish and even anger against God, before expressing trust and confidence in him as well – and they do so in the context of public worship.

I believe that one of the challenges that the Church needs to face is to allow the expression of grief felt by a family at a funeral as well as offering hope in the midst of it. Jesus' example shows us how grief can be expressed.

2. The Psalms

The singing and recital of psalms has an older pedigree than any other form of sung worship. Most of the psalms were written nearly 2500 years ago, and some may well be older: all have been recited in Jewish and Christian worship since that time. it is therefore unsurprising that we are commended to use them in our funeral services too – the pity is that their use is becoming fairly infrequent.

The psalms fall into two main categories – psalms of lament and psalms of thanksgiving. I wish to consider in particular the former category as an aid to worship in funerals. They contain some of the most astonishing words in the whole of Scripture: words in which the writer is prepared to rail against God. Consider Jesus' quotation of Psalm 22:1: 'My God, my God, why have you forsaken me?' or the opening verse of Psalm 60: 'O God, you have rejected us, broken our defences; you have been angry; now restore us!'

In the last 100 years there has been a great deal of scholarship by Christian theologians on the nature of the psalms. Most commentators refer back to the influence of the German theologian Hermann Gunkel, who wrote nearly a century ago. In recent times, though, his compatriot Claus Westermann, as well as the American Presbyterian writer, Walter Brueggemann, have been particularly significant.[23]

Many of the psalms begin with a plea to God to hear them – the opening of both psalms cited above are examples. They express a sentiment that is often felt by people in times of crisis, yet the Church has been reticent in allowing this to be uttered in worship. If people express the thought that God has abandoned them, it is too easy to tell them quickly that that is not the case and that God is with them in the darkest valleys. The psalmist knows that to be true, yet he is not afraid to utter his darkest thoughts as part of a prayer to God. We should allow people to do the same.

There are two significant aspects to the psalms of lament which are useful and instructive for us. The first is the willingness to express the sorrow felt – the psalmist feels that God has abandoned him, or that he is in a deep pit and longs for God to rescue him (such as Psalm 130:1), or that he is surrounded by his enemies who curse and deride him (Psalm 102:8). As we saw when we considered Jesus' use of Psalm 22, these words were written to be spoken in corporate worship. There is no sense that it is all right to have these private thoughts but we do better to keep them to ourselves: these words of despair would be spoken by the congregation together. Surely, at a funeral, there will be people who could echo that sense of abandonment by God in their hearts, or feel that they are crying out to God from the depths. Should we not allow liturgical expression of the feelings of the bereaved at some point in the service?

However, just as significant within the psalms of lament is the other key feature: they do not end the psalm on the same note of despair with which they start. There is a movement within each psalm (with the notable exception of Psalm 88) from complaint to praise. So Psalm 22, which begins with the psalmist feeling he has been abandoned by God, moves by verse 21b to an acknowledgement that God has rescued him, and the psalmist states that he will praise God in the midst of the people in the congregation. The psalms of lament are characterised as much by praise of God and trust in him, but that praise and trust is nearly always expressed only after the psalmist has been able to express his fear and pain.

So how should the Psalms be used in funerals? The most well-known of them, Psalm 23, is usually used in the metrical Psalm version, 'The Lord's My Shepherd', sung to the tune of Crimond.

---

23. For those readers who want to delve deeper into the structure of the psalms and the influence of psalms of lament, the key studies are Gunkel's 1926 commentary on the Psalms, and, in more recent years, Claus Westermann, *Praise and Lament in the Psalms*, Edinburgh: T & T Clark, 1981. Brueggemann's work, *The Message of the Psalms*, Minneapolis: Augsberg Publishing House, 1984, combines rigorous scholarship with easy accessibility for the lay person.

Although it can be characterised as a psalm of lament, what comes through most strongly is the expression of trust in God rather than complaint against him. Nonetheless, its recognition of the journey through the darkest valley, and of the psalmist's enemies amongst whom God prepares a table, means that this can be properly characterised as a psalm of lament. It recognises the place of pain in people's lives and expresses trust in the midst of it.

However, other uses can be made of the Psalms within a funeral. It can be difficult for mourners to express some of the pain they feel, but there is a place for the officiating minister to do that for them in a liturgical setting. Alongside – or perhaps in place of some of the more confident opening sentences – some verses from psalms of lament could be used. Words such as Psalm 130:1-2 – 'Out of the depths I cry to you, O Lord. Lord, hear my voice' – may reflect more accurately the emotions felt by the mourners than words of reassurance that nothing can separate us from God's love, or even that those who believe in Jesus as the resurrection and the life will never die. The mourners will be certain that their loved one has, in fact, died.

In 1996, Nicholas Wolsterstorff wrote a book entitled *Lament for a Son* in which he told the story of his son, Eric, who had died in a skiing accident aged only 25. The book is a searing and honest account of the emotions felt and the faith sustained in the face of an awful tragedy. What the author pleads for most of all is for people not to tell him that everything will be all right. He felt that things were awful, and he needed that to be acknowledged. He writes:

> Death is awful, demonic. If you think your task as comforter is to tell me that really, all things considered, it's not so bad, you do not sit with me in my grief but place yourself off in the distance from me. Over there, you are of no help. What I need to hear from you is that you recognise how painful it is. I need to hear from you that you are with me in my desperation. To comfort me, you have to come close. Come sit beside me on my mourning bench.[24]

The Church lets people down when it refuses to sit beside them on their mourning bench. We have learnt that we have to do that in the time leading up to the funeral, but it can often feel that in the funeral service itself we must ignore the grief that is felt and speak only of hope and reasons for thanksgiving. The Psalms offer so many resources to speak and sing out the pain that is felt, and it is a great shame when they are not used. Wolsterstorff commissioned a requiem to be written for his son: in it, he follows the pattern of the psalmist in allowing words of Scripture which speak out the pain and anguish

---

24. Nicholas Wolsterstorff, *Lament for a Son*, Grand Rapids: Eerdmans, 1996, p.34.

against God, before speaking words of trust and thanksgiving by the end. There will be few families whom we encounter at the point of bereavement who will be in a position to commission a requiem, yet part of our task as Christian ministers is to enable the words of pain to be spoken in the presence of God in worship.

The power of the Psalms lies in their expression of faith in the midst of pain still real. Their use at a funeral gives voice to grief and to hope.

3. Bible readings

In the first English Prayer Book of 1549, after the priest had met the coffin in the churchyard and had recited the opening words of Scripture, the rubric indicates that a Bible reading was to be read. The accompanying notes of guidance suggest that it 'may be taken out of the fifteenth chapter of the First Epistle of the Corinthians'. By the time of the 1662 Church of England prayer book, this was the set Bible reading for the burial of the dead. It is a wonderful passage, full of great promises reminding us that 'death is swallowed up in victory'. It asks the rhetorical questions which Handel sets to music so powerfully in *The Messiah*: 'O death, where is thy sting? O grave, where is thy victory?'

However, we should acknowledge that this reading from 1 Corinthians is not exactly easy to follow and is very long. Even if we read it in a modern translation rather than the King James Version, or the version which is set in the Book of Common Prayer, Paul's arguments are not straightforward. Indeed, it is precisely because he is in the middle of an argument with the people of Corinth that it is difficult to understand! There were some people in the early Church in Corinth who suggested that there was no resurrection of the dead, and it is this suggestion that Paul is seeking to counter. Of course, there are parallels today – there will be many people gathered at a funeral who do not believe in any notion of a life after death, let alone have a Christian understanding of the resurrection of the body. Nonetheless, I think that there are so many constraints on a minister in his or her preaching at a funeral that there is insufficient time to give full weight to Paul's argument, and I fear that this long reading would leave many mourners baffled.

There are, of course, many alternatives. At a time of grief and bereavement, great comfort can be found in the familiar: if the family has a favourite and familiar passage of Scripture, that may be a good reason to use it. Examples may include Psalm 23 'The Lord is My Shepherd', the Beatitudes from Matthew 5, or St Paul's hymn to love in 1 Corinthians 13. Sadly today, there are many people in this country who could not name any passage of Scripture, so here are some possibilities that are also frequently used at funerals.

1. Ecclesiastes 3:1-11: 'For everything there is a season.' It is notable that of all the suggested Bible readings listed by the Church of England, this is not one of them! However, I am often asked for this passage at funerals – maybe people remember it from the famous adaptation of it by The Byrds in the 1960s, 'Turn! Turn! Turn!' The Book of Ecclesiastes is one of the most extraordinary in the whole of Scripture, because the writer seems so gloomy about everything! He considers life and all its workings and dismisses most of it as mere vanity! Certainly, this Bible passage contains none of the riches of some of the Gospel readings that will be considered below and yet, even within the writer's despair at life, he recognises the place of God. Ecclesiastes 3 offers a vision of the world which is ordered and where there is a time for everything: undoubtedly, a funeral is a time to mourn, and this passage gives permission for that. Moreover, in the weeks and months following bereavement, it can feel as though chaos threatens to overwhelm the mourners, and this passage can be a reminder of the hope of order.
2. John 14:1-6: This is one of the most commonly used passages of Scripture today, with its reassuring reminder that Jesus is the way, the truth and the life and the way to God. In Chapter 2 I mentioned the story of the clergyperson who didn't feel it right to include the words, 'No one comes to the father except through me', for fear of offending people of other faiths. And yet, at a funeral conducted by a Christian minister, it seems odd to bowdlerise Scripture in this way. Undoubtedly, this phrase has been used as a weapon against people of other faiths, and that is to be condemned, yet that is not a reason not to use the passage. Jesus is about to die, and he paints a picture of travelling a journey to a distant house where the householder awaits us with open arms and hospitality. Often memories of a loved one centre around the house where she or he lived for many years and, pastorally, I have found it helpful to be able to say that the promise of Scripture is that there is another house now for the one who has died – a house with God in heaven. John 14:27 is often added at the end of verse 6 at a funeral: 'Peace I leave with you; my peace I give to you . . . Do not let your hearts be troubled and do not let them be afraid.' These last words pick up the opening words of Chapter 14, and so the peace of God is emphasised at a time of great turmoil.
3. Revelation 21:1-6: I find this passage particularly suitable when someone has died after a long or debilitating illness. It paints a picture of a world where there is no more sickness, no more pain,

no more death – in other words, a world where those things which have torn the family apart in the death of their loved one will be no more. It describes these things as 'the first things' and offers completion of the story of the world which began at Creation and was then disrupted at the Fall. Finally, by the Book of Revelation, that disruption has come to an end and all is restored to how it was at the beginning of Creation. Most of all, like the passage from John 14, it offers a vision of a life lived with God.

There are, of course, many other suitable passages of Scripture which may have particular relevance to the family. Although I expressed some anxiety about the opening sentences proclaiming too confidently the hope that we have through the death and resurrection of Christ, this is certainly not an anxiety that we should allow to affect us in our choice of Bible reading. In the reading of Scripture during the service, our chief concern should be to ensure that we offer people hope: we believe that death is not simply an end, but a new beginning which can be lived with God.

Non-biblical readings

It is fairly common now when a minister goes to speak to a family about organising a funeral that they will want a particular poem or piece of prose read as part of the service. It may have been included in a condolences card which they were sent, or perhaps someone in the family will have heard it read at another funeral and it struck a chord. Any anthology of funeral readings – or indeed a perusal of the internet on the subject – will reveal a vast number of suitable readings. The most common is still undoubtedly Henry Scott Holland's 'Death is nothing at all' which I discussed in Chapter 2, but there are many other alternatives.

I touched on the dilemma faced by ministers over this matter in Chapter 1. How do we assess whether or not to include items requested by the family? We may want to dismiss some offerings as simply bad poetry, but clearly that is not a reason to refuse them! Paul Sheppy expresses it well when considering whether or not to allow these requests:

> To allow all the family requires may obscure the Christ whose death encompasses all human death. To deny the family may equally obscure the Christ who came not for the righteous but for sinners – of whom the Church is, of course, comprised.[25]

---

25. Ibid, p.8.

HEAVEN'S MORNING BREAKS

I want to offer brief reflections on two non-biblical readings which are often read at funerals – one of which offers false comfort, the other of which can be read in the light of Jesus' words of hope.

'Do not stand at my grave and weep' by Mary Elizabeth Fry

Do not stand at my grave and weep.
I am not there. I do not sleep.
I am a thousand winds that blow.
I am the diamond glints on snow.
I am the sunlight on ripened grain.
I am the gentle autumn rain.
When you awaken in the morning's hush
I am the swift uplifting rush
of quiet birds in circled flight.
I am the soft stars that shine at night.
Do not stand at my grave and cry;
I am not there. I did not die.

This is undoubtedly one of the most popular poems to be read at a funeral. It could be said to offer hope to the family: its central message is that death is not the end for the deceased and that there is life beyond the grave. The nature of that life, however, seems extraordinary: taken literally, it suggests a sort of life where upon our death we melt into nature and become part of all that is around us. Taken figuratively, it need only mean that the wind and the stars and quiet birds act as triggers to flood our minds with memories. Whilst people find it increasingly difficult to believe in an orthodox Christian understanding of life beyond the grave, this poem colludes with a very different vision.

More troubling, perhaps, is the poem's attitude towards death. The opening and closing couplets both attempt to deny the reality of death, which would suggest that there is no need to go through any rite of separation or transition because death is not real. But this is not the Christian message. We acknowledge that death is real because we follow a founder who died and for whom his close friends and family mourned deeply. A poem such as Fry's undermines the validity of grief and appears to deny any separation.

'The ship' by Bishop Charles Brent

I am standing on the sea shore.
A ship sails in the morning breeze and starts for the ocean.
She is an object of beauty and I stand watching her
till at last she fades on the horizon and someone at my side says:
'She is gone.'

> Gone! Where? Gone from my sight – that is all.
> She is just as large in the masts, hull and spars as she was when
> I saw her
> and just as able to bear her load of living freight to its destination.
> The diminished size and total loss of sight is in me, not in her.
>
> And just at the moment when someone at my side says,
> 'She is gone,' there are others who are watching her coming, and other
> voices take up a glad shout: 'There she comes' – and that is dying.

This reading is sometimes attributed to Victor Hugo from his novel *Toilers of the Sea*, but is generally said to be written by Charles Brent, a nineteenth-century bishop in the Philippines. It fits well with an understanding of the funeral as a transition rite of passage, and indeed of death as the final part of our earthly pilgrimage from this place into the arms of God. It does not undermine Christian notions of the resurrection of the body in the way that the first poem does, and speaks eloquently of a worldview in which the living and the dead are two communities, separate and yet alongside each other. Whilst it does not give full expression to the reality of grief in death, it does not diminish the reality of separation that death brings.

The danger with many readings is that they aim to offer comfort by denying reality. I suspect people like the thought of them because they do not like the process of grief. However, as ministers, we are called to offer hope in the midst of pain, not to suggest that the pain need not be expressed.

Conclusion

Readings from the Bible – and often, nowadays, from other sources – form the backbone of most funeral services conducted by Christian ministers. Their words allow us to lift our eyes from the circumstances of this particular family and this particular death to see what is said about death in general and to hear words of hope that have stood for thousands of years. The wonderful thing about Scripture is that it gives voice to our sorrow as much as providing a reason for our hope. I think a Christian funeral should address both aspects of this honestly, allowing the grief that is felt to find expression, as well as offering hope in the midst of a family's pain.

Four
A time to speak

The eulogy and address

It is tempting for a commentator on funerals to see funeral eulogies as a relatively recent phenomenon. As I said in Chapter 1, many people point to the funeral of Diana, Princess of Wales, at which her brother Earl Spencer gave a moving tribute, as the moment when people began to insist on there being a personal account of a person's life by a family member or friend as part of the funeral ritual. Certainly, during the 15 years that I have been ordained, there has been a marked shift from services where I, as officiating minister, included in my sermon a brief outline of the person's life as a form of eulogy, to services today where this is most rare and there is almost always someone who knew the person well who will do this.

Undoubtedly, there has been a move towards more 'person-centred' funerals that focus far more on the life of the deceased and make it personal to him or her. In the Church of England, it was not until the liturgical revisions which followed the Liturgical Commission of 1965 that the deceased was actually mentioned by name in the formal liturgy! Up to that point, the priest could get away with simply referring to 'our dear brother' or 'dear sister'. In a society with a high mortality rate, death was too frequent an occurrence to focus on each individual death by name. Nowadays, death is much more hidden away, but when it comes, society expects the focus to be on the person who has died.

When it came to eulogies, most Church traditions also used to be fairly clear that they were not to be encouraged, for the simple reason that the focus of the funeral then became the life of the deceased rather than the hope of the gospel. Where eulogies are commonplace, it can take a courageous minister to insist on offering another spoken address in which the gospel is preached. However, when a funeral does not have a sermon or homily which offers a prospective focus of the hope of resurrection in balance to the retrospective thanksgiving for the person's life, the gospel message is obscured.

Despite the strictures on funeral eulogies, they have a long pedigree. Thomas Long points to the example of the seventeenth-century French priest, Jacques Bossuet (1627–1704), as the 'most celebrated Christian funeral sermoniser in history'.[26] He was chaplain to the court of the

---

26. Long, *Accompany them with Singing*, p.183.

Sun King, Louis XIV, and was frequently called upon to preach on the occasions of royal funerals. As a conscientious priest, he endeavoured to offer a gospel message alongside a brief outline of the person's life.

On one occasion, he was called upon to give the funeral oration for a particularly notorious liver called Anne of Gonzaga. To make matters worse, she had published a memoir of her life shortly before death, confessing all in gory detail. If good manners prevented people from speaking ill of the dead, it seemed that there would be little that poor Jacques Bossuet could say about her! However, he found a way round his problem. He opened his sermon by painting the scene of a remarkable conversion that Anne had encountered late in life – even later, happily, than the publication of her lurid memoirs! Thus, in the style of so many testimonies today, he was able to outline in great detail the shocking sins of her life before accounting how God's grace was greater than her wretchedness and how she ended her days a sinner saved by divine providence. Many of the congregation remained doubtful as to the historical accuracy of the deathbed conversion, though, of course, they were delighted to hear all the details of her sin![27]

Bossuet's problem underlines one of the difficulties that those preaching at funerals face today, which will be discussed below: when we know very little about the faith of the deceased, should we make claims about it or promises to the congregation about the eternal destination of the deceased?

Given that it is much rarer nowadays for eulogies to be given by the officiating minister, the dilemma faced by the clergy concerns how to manage the tributes that other people give. Most of us have attended a funeral where a tribute has been given that has gone on for far too long, or is inaudible, or attempts to paint a picture of a plaster saint, which may well not be how we remember the person! Sometimes there are even three or four separate tributes, with each person determined to say all that they knew of the deceased. If the whole service is to take place at the crematorium chapel, the length of the eulogy is particularly important because it is likely that there will be another funeral scheduled to start 45 or even 30 minutes later. If a eulogy goes on too long, it is very difficult for the minister to try and make up time in the rest of the service in a way that does not leave the family wondering why the second part of the funeral was so rushed!

However, there are great advantages to a tribute from a family member, too. It will be far more personal than anything offered by the minister; the person paying the tribute is likely to be better known to the mourners which will increase the sense of personalisation for them.

---

27. Ibid, p.184f.

There is, of course, the danger that the person paying the tribute will break down, but is that so terrible? It is a funeral, after all! If one of its purposes is to mourn, a demonstration of that grief will not feel so out of place. Naturally, a wise minister will have a back-up plan and should be able to take over reading a written script as appropriate, but I do not believe that a family member should be excluded from giving a tribute because they may get upset.

Paul Sheppy's words about obscuring the Christ we want to proclaim seem pertinent when it comes to tributes too. Our role is not simply to provide beautiful liturgy or offer a moving farewell: it is to walk with the family at the time of their grief and work with them in allowing the funeral to be a time when they say goodbye to a loved one in a way that honours them. If we simply refuse all family tributes, what will be remembered after the service – however well we conduct the rest of it – is that the minister would not allow them to speak. One young man wanted to read a poem at a funeral at which I officiated for his grandfather and commented, 'I would never forgive myself if I couldn't do this for Granddad.' This sentiment sums up exactly the desire in many people's hearts at funerals these days. There will be many people who recognise straight away that they would be unable to do it, but when people feel that they can, and would like to, clergy need to show patience and understanding in the face of this desire.

The length of a eulogy is, of course, an issue. Few people who give them have any training or background in public speaking, and it can be difficult to hold people's attention. However, pastoral considerations also apply here. In the USA, party planners are now getting in on the funeral act; one event organiser, John Leland, commented peevishly that 'it doesn't matter how much you loved someone, after you've heard someone drone on for five minutes, you're annoyed. It's about poignant moments. Maudlin is not poignant.'[28] Harsh words! My advice to Mr Leland is to get out of the funeral business – if you can't listen to a tribute about someone's life for more than five minutes, you are going to have some very annoying moments!

On those occasions where nobody in the family feels able to give a tribute, it is important that the minister says something about the person's life. I quoted Paul Sheppy in Chapter 1 when he describes a funeral as 'primarily a remembrance of this person's death in the context of the Easter event'.[29] While it is vital that the message of Easter comes through, part of remembering this person's death is reminding ourselves of some of the facts and memories around his or her life.

There are a number of pointers which are helpful:

---

28. John Leland, 'It's my funeral and I'll serve ice cream if I want to', *New York Times*, 20 July 2006.
29. Sheppy, *Death Liturgy and Ritual, Vol 1*, p.8.

1. Timing: If we are concerned that tributes paid by family members might go on too long, we should pay them the same respect by not offering our own eulogy of great length. I suspect that about five minutes about the person is quite long enough.
2. Personal memories: If you knew the person at all, offer your own memories. There is a danger attached to this: do not pretend to know someone you have scarcely met! People often express the unease about leaving a funeral where the vicar has talked about someone as though they were a dear friend, when the reality is they did not know each other. However, if there are personal memories that you do have, it can be a powerful way to connect with the mourners by speaking about these.
3. Evoke other people's memories: When I do not know the person who has died at all, I find it helpful to suggest that people think about their own memories as I outline the facts of the person's life. So I might begin by saying at the funeral of an elderly person, 'Perhaps there are a few of you here today who still remember Molly's childhood,' and take the opportunity to outline some of the facts of Molly's childhood – where she was born, how many brothers and sisters she had, what she did when she left school, and so on. I find that I can then say something similar for different periods of a person's life – when they had a young family, their work life, their retirement. In this way, our words act as a trigger to other people's memories rather than claiming to have those memories for ourself. I conducted a funeral recently where the deceased's elderly sister kept calling out from the congregation to tell me that I had got my facts wrong and to provide me with the correct information. I had been relying on what I had been told by the lady's children, but they clearly were not the most accurate sources! At the end of the service, as I rather sheepishly apologised to mourners for not having the right information, they all smiled – the deceased would have behaved in exactly the same way as her sister, so it rather put them in mind of her!
4. Don't just rely on facts: Some of the most boring eulogies that I have heard simply outline the facts of a person's life and leave it at that. Facts are important to frame a person's life, but much more important in a eulogy are the little memories that call them to mind. A rhetorical question thrown out, asking what words sum up the person, allows the congregation to spend time with their own memories. I offer a few suggestions in a eulogy – her garden; Arsenal FC; time spent with the grandchildren, for example. Some of the words may be painful ones – cantankerous may well be the first word that springs to mind for some people! We should not be afraid to allow people to think those thoughts: a eulogy

which does nothing but speak of a person in glowing terms renders that person little more than a plaster saint. Most of us would hate to be thought of like that, so we should not do it to those who have died.

I have often found that by giving people permission to remember the bad things as well as the good, we have a greater opportunity as ministers then to speak to them of the Christian hope. At the heart of our faith is the belief that 'while we were still sinners Christ died for us' (Romans 5:8), so we can confidently proclaim a message that offers hope and healing to our failures and despair. This does not give us permission in the style of Bossuet at Anne Gonzaga's funeral to outline the lurid details of a person's life: it is enough simply to acknowledge that we all come with strengths and weaknesses, and that God's grace is sufficient to redeem our failures.

It is vital that when we are asked to offer a personal tribute to someone as part of the address, we should not limit our words to speaking about that person. Sheppy's words that the funeral sets the person's life in the context of Easter reminds us that we should speak of the hope that springs from Easter. Nowadays, we are often not asked to give the tribute because someone else will do so; this should free us in our address to concentrate solely on the gospel message.

The purpose of the sermon or homily is to remind people that funerals do not just have a retrospective focus. When funerals are conducted by civil celebrants or humanist ministers, they are very clear that that is what the service is for. In other words, its purpose is to remind ourselves of the person who has died and to give thanks for their life. They may be able to say that the person who has died lives on in the memories of those who mourn, but they cannot say that the deceased lives on in any objective reality. I fear that services conducted by Christian ministers where there is no homily separate from a eulogy spoken by a family friend give insufficient weight to the prospective hope that counterbalances the retrospective thanksgiving.

As Christians, we have a different story to tell. The homily therefore provides a helpful balance to the eulogy and encourages people to look forward with hope as well as back with thanksgiving. For this reason, I think the homily should always come towards the end of the service, after personal tributes and poems have been read. Psychologically, I think it is easier for the family members to know that their contributions will come early in the service so that they can give themselves time to grieve and break down if they need do within the service, rather than needing to hold it together to give their speech. There is a theological and liturgical reason for this too: we should leave the service having offered hope as the final word.

The greatest dilemma facing the minister is what sort of hope should be offered to the family. If we are accepted by God and welcomed into his family on the basis of our faith in the death and resurrection of Jesus Christ, what hope do we offer to families where the deceased did not appear to have a faith in Jesus?

The answer to this question will undoubtedly depend on where we stand on the issues explored in Chapter 2 on the effect of Christ's death in the world. If we are clear that Christ died as a substitute for our sins, then unless I accept that he was a substitute for me, it is hard to see how I can benefit from it. If I believe that Christ died as a representative of humanity, then his representative death affected the whole of humanity and effected a change in the standing of humanity before God. It is possible then to speak more confidently about any death, as all deaths are transformed into life through Jesus.

In Chapter 2, I offered an alternative based on the writing of the Swiss theologian von Balthasar, whereby even in death we have the opportunity to respond to the Christ who was with the dead in hell and even from hell could rescue those with him there.

Christians have disagreed politely – and indeed violently – with each other as to the meaning of Christ's death. I do not intend to say who is right and who is wrong. If the minister holds to a substitutionary view of the Atonement, she or he will need to be cautious about how the hope of the Christian faith is expressed. Perhaps it should be enough to caution that none of us knows the state of other people's hearts or their standing before God – clearly mourners will be very upset if the minister says something like, 'Sadly, it is too late for David to put himself right before God, but you have the chance to change, and you should do so if you do not want to go to hell as he has!' This is, of course, a parody of the very worst sort of preaching, yet ministers do need to be very careful about making statements that appear to judge other people's eternal destiny.

It is possible to speak of God's welcome and hospitality to all. We can express the central Christian hope that if we put our belief and trust in God in this life, he will welcome us in the next. That leaves the unspoken implication that if we do not put our trust in God in this life, he will not welcome us – but at least it is unspoken. I do not believe that it is our role as ministers to tell grieving families that it is too late for their loved one and that God has not welcomed them. We also need not say that we will see the deceased again one day – none of us know what form our resurrection bodies will take.

Preaching at funerals is not straightforward, but it should be done. We should not leave it to families simply to offer a eulogy of their loved one: our task is to offer hope. How that hope is expressed will depend on our own theology, but I believe we have failed a family if they leave a funeral service which has not spelt out that hope in the words offered by the minister.

Prayers

The other main form of spoken word in a Christian funeral are the prayers. Prayer transforms a funeral because it reminds us that there are not simply two parties to a funeral – the minister and the mourners. It would be possible to conduct a funeral which is in effect a conversation between two sides. On the one side is the person leading, with contributions from people speaking about the person; on the other are those listening to the tributes. It is an entirely human affair; an acknowledgement that 'this life is all there is', and therefore at a funeral all we can do is to allow people in this life to have a conversation with others here about someone who is no longer in this life. We could even include words from the Bible, and they may be regarded as Wisdom of the Ancients, but they will be no better than other wise words of philosophy.

I do not wish to dismiss funerals which do this: the increasing popularity of services conducted by civil celebrants and other officials suggest that many find great comfort in services where there is no prayer. And, of course, music connects with the human spirit in a way beyond words: any funeral can acknowledge that we are not simply mind and body, but spirit too. However, to include prayers in a service recognises a different dimension: in short, prayer directly brings God into our funerals. Prayer is not addressed to the mourners in the way that readings and eulogies are: it is addressed to God.

I consider the various types of prayer at a funeral below, but want to say a few words first about intercessory prayer – that is, praying for others, or asking God to meet our own needs. It is only one form of prayer that we encounter in a funeral, but it is helpful to consider what it is we are doing with such prayer.

The most helpful understanding of this kind of prayer that I have ever found is to see it as a triangle of love – a triangle between the person praying, the person being prayed for and God. What joins the three points of the triangle is love. You may think that we should pray for everyone rather than just those we love, but surely the point that Jesus makes is that we should love our enemy and see the whole world as our neighbour: in prayer, we bring them all into that triangle of love. Even when we pray for ourselves, our prayer should be motivated by having a third person in mind. When we pray that we would see life as a blessing, not a burden, we pray that we would see those around us with love – that they would become the third point of the triangle, as it were. If we pray that God would help us to look after our families, it is our families who occupy that third point. If we pray that God would make us rich and successful, we have to question whether we are trying to cover two bases of the triangle ourselves, and whether that is valid prayer!

A funeral without prayer may thus be seen thus:

Minister _____ Deceased _____ Mourners

Of course, love is still present here; it can still be love that motivates the conversation about the one who has died. But prayer brings in a different dimension.

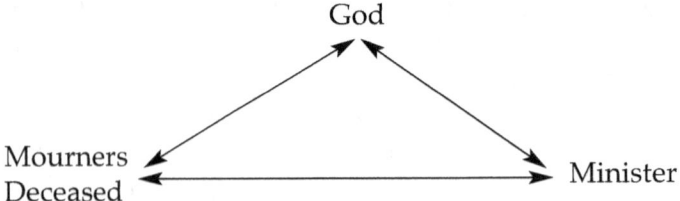

It is notable that often when a civil celebrant conducts a funeral, the family will still want to say the Lord's Prayer, even if they do not want any other prayers. Even in a world where we are told that only that which is scientifically verifiable can be accepted as true, we long to reach out to another dimension and acknowledge the presence of God. The familiar words of the Lord's Prayer allow people to do this.

Before I consider particular points of prayer within the funeral service, there is a pressing question to consider:

Should Christians pray for the dead?

You will see that in my diagram above, I have placed the deceased alongside the mourners at one point in the triangle. Some Christians will be very uncomfortable with that, believing that we should no longer pray for the dead because they are either in the hands of God, in which case they need no more prayer, or they are not, in which case it is too late for them to need prayer!

However, if we consider prayer to be a triangle of love, we do not cease to love a person because they are no longer alive. I considered this issue in a little more detail in Chapter 1 when we looked at who the funeral was for. As Christians, we state in the Apostles' Creed that we believe in the Communion of Saints: this includes those who have died and are now with God. Prayer is far more than simply asking God for things: it is about acknowledging his presence and our communion with him alongside others whom we love. Seen in this light, it is entirely appropriate to include those who have now died – particularly at a funeral service!

In the view of salvation outlined in Chapter 2 where Christ can still rescue those who are dead because he was present himself amongst them, it makes good theological sense to pray for the dead. If, even in death, people can know the light and love of Christ because Christ was present among the dead on Holy Saturday, it seems right that we pray for those whom we love, that they would still be aware of that love in death and respond to it. 1 Peter 3:19 talks about Jesus preaching the good news to those spirits that are dead: if God is outside human time, could this verse not also apply to those people who came after him as well as before?

This does not address the question of whether we should pray *to* the dead, whether they are saints of old, or even Jesus' mother Mary. That is a different question, which will certainly bring even more disagreement amongst Christians! As it is not directly relevant to a book on funerals, I am not going to address it here.

There are three key moments within a funeral service for prayer:

1. At the beginning of the service or after the first hymn. Often there are prayers of confession at this stage.
2. Intercessions: we pray for those who mourn and give thanks for the deceased and include the deceased in our prayers. Often the Lord's Prayer is said at this point.
3. Commendation: we pray to God to welcome the departed in his love.

1. Prayers at the beginning of the service

By including prayer near the beginning of a funeral service, we acknowledge from the beginning that the service is not simply a conversation between humans: we recognise the presence of God amongst us. An opening prayer will frequently ask God to comfort those who mourn: if the opening sentences have been full of words declaring our hope and trust, I think it is important to recognise the grief that is part of the service too.

Some ministers will always include a prayer of confession in the service. If the funeral is a Requiem Mass within the Catholic tradition, or otherwise includes Communion, the service would always include the opportunity for confession, to ensure that we come to the Communion rail with clean hands and a clean heart. Even when it is not a Communion service, there may well be good reason to include a simple confession near the beginning of the service.

Some may feel that this underlines an unhelpful preoccupation of the church with guilt and sin, but I think that is an unfair accusation. I recall one minister, who always includes a prayer of confession in his funeral services, commenting to me, 'I don't always know why I include a confession, but I normally find that someone in the congregation does.' Those who work with the bereaved often find that there are feelings of guilt surrounding their relationship with the deceased: things they wish we hadn't said or done, or perhaps anger about actions taken by the deceased towards them.

To include a confession in the service frees the mourners from the burden of making the funeral a celebration only of the good. Sometimes the children of a much-loved member of the community can come to a funeral service as aware of how he let them down as a father as they are of his wonderful contribution to community life. It can be very difficult in those circumstances if tributes and eulogies only speak of what a wonderful man he was, and the uppermost thought in his children's minds is how he let them down.

A confession spoken by the minister on behalf of the congregation recognises before God that the dead person, loved as he or she was, also got it wrong. It also recognises that there will be those in the congregation who failed on occasion in their relationship with the one who has died.

When the Scottish Episcopal Church came to draft a new service in the 1980s, it consulted Dr Colin Murray-Parkes, one of the world's authorities on bereavement and loss. I think these prayers of confession, spoken by the minister on behalf of everyone, capture very well the two sides that need to be expressed:

> Forgiving God,
> in the face of death we discover
> how many things are still undone,
> how much might have been done otherwise.
> Redeem our failure.
> Bind up the wounds of past mistakes.
> Transform our guilt to active love,
> and by your forgiveness make us whole.
>
> God our Redeemer,
> you love all that you have made,
> you are merciful beyond our deserving.
> Pardon your servant's sins,
> acknowledged or unperceived.
> Help us also to forgive as we pray to be forgiven,
> through him who on the cross
> asked forgiveness for those who wounded him.
> Through Jesus Christ our Lord. Amen

An alternative in churches with a tradition of set liturgies is to use the words of the *Kyrie Eleison* – Lord, have mercy. In this way, the minister can use three sentences with words of confession – often taken from penitential psalms such as Psalm 130 or Psalm 51 – and concludes each sentence with 'Lord, have mercy' or 'Christ, have mercy'. The congregation then repeat 'Lord, have mercy'. This form of confession works where there is a significant number in the congregation who are used to this format and are confident about joining in with the responses.

2. Prayers of intercession

Prayers of intercession, as I indicated above, express the love felt for those prayed for. There is an opportunity in the prayers to give thanks for the deceased person's life, so it makes sense that these prayers follow the eulogies, so that those gathered will have in mind memories of that person. We pray for those who mourn, naming them before God. If ministers are uncomfortable about including a proper confession earlier in the service, there is the opportunity in the intercessions to acknowledge painful memories and to pray for forgiveness for them. There are also many prayers which can be expressed here, which acknowledge that we too are mortal and heading towards our own death, so we pray for the strength to face the future and faith to live in the light of eternity.

Finally, and vitally, if there has not been an opportunity to pray the words of the Lord's Prayer at the funeral, it should be included at this point. This allows the congregation to give expression to words of prayer themselves, so that they are included in the praying, rather than that simply being the domain of the minister. I think that the traditional words of the Lord's Prayer should nearly always be used at a funeral. There are few things that upset people more at a church funeral than finding themselves tripping up over words which they thought were familiar, but whose rhythms have changed to suit modern language. There may be many good reasons for the Church to have a modern version of the Lord's Prayer, but when most of the population is still familiar with the traditional words, it is that very familiarity that provides important comfort at a time of distress. We may be coming to a time when most people no longer know the Lord's Prayer, in which case it may not matter which version of the prayer is used. However, at the moment, I think ministers should err on the side of tradition.

A few other comments about the content of the prayers of intercession:

a. Allow for silence: In a Quaker funeral service, any prayers of intercession would be expected to be offered silently. As I said at the start of the chapter, that can be liberating and healing. A time of prayer can offer a wonderful opportunity in any funeral to give a time for silence so that people can offer their own prayers to God, or simply be still. It is extraordinary how powerful silence can be. I have found, particularly at funerals where there are very few mourners, that silence can have a transformative effect.

b. Use of names: When we pray for those who mourn, it is important to name them. God calls each of us by name and our names matter to him. To name the chief mourners in prayer is a reminder that they, too, are known to him by name. At this point in the service, the minister is very vulnerable if she or he has not met the family prior to the person's death. You are reliant on the family to give you the correct information and on writing it down correctly! Asking for all the family's names may also reveal deep family hurts and reveal family feuds which need to be handled with great care. The family may tell you that there is another son or daughter of the deceased, but they have no contact with the rest of the family; or there are grandchildren who have no contact with their father or mother, and thereby lost contact also with the grandparents. Should they be included in the prayers by name? What about a divorced daughter-in-law or son-in-law who remained close to their mother-in-law, even though the son or daughter remarried? Which partner should be included? There are no easy answers, but the minister needs to be aware of them. Personally, I think the task of including people by name in the prayers is so important as to take the risk, but it is essential to be aware of the risk.

3. Prayers of commendation

Towards the end of the funeral service, there are prayers of commendation which name the deceased again to God and entrust them to God's loving mercy. I discussed this in Chapter 1, when we considered who the funeral was for. Protestant traditions – including the rite of the Church of England for many centuries in the *Book of Common Prayer* – did not include a commendation, for the reasons that I outlined earlier: if the person was already dead, nothing could be said at the time of his funeral that would affect whether or not God would take him to be with him in heaven. However, for the reasons given in Chapter 1, I think there are good reasons to include a commendation, and I think the modern Church of England rite is justified in including it.

One of the most moving prayers of commendation is undoubtedly the Eastern Orthodox Kontakion for the deceased, which dates back as far as the sixth century AD and is still used today in Orthodox funeral rites. There are various forms of the words used in English: the following are a translation of the words used in a hymn sung in the Orthodox Church in Ukraine (the music of which, incidentally, was used over the opening credits of David Lean's film, *Doctor Zhivago*!):

> Give rest, O Christ, to thy servant with thy saints:
> where sorrow and pain are no more;
> neither sighing but life everlasting.
> Thou only art immortal, the creator and maker of man:
> and we are mortal formed from the dust of the earth,
> and unto earth shall we return:
> for so thou didst ordain,
> when thou created me saying:
> 'Dust thou art and unto dust shalt thou return.'
> All we go down to the dust;
> and weeping o'er the grave we make our song:
> Alleluia, alleluia, alleluia.

The power of these words at a funeral lie in their recognition of the sorrow and awfulness of the situation, whilst still expressing hope and trust in God. 'Weeping o'er the grave we make our song: Alleluia', encapsulates both the grief we feel over the loss of a loved one and the hope that enables us to sing 'Alleluia' as a declaration of trust and thanksgiving in Almighty God.

As I said at the start of Chapter 3, a funeral service is full of words. The writer E. M. Forster once dismissed our faith as 'poor, little talkative Christianity'.[30] A focus on words should not blind us to the power of silence, music and symbol. However, neither should we dismiss spoken words. We follow a Saviour who was described as the Word made flesh, and in the words we offer to those in need, hope is proclaimed and love expressed.

---

30. E. M. Forster, *A Passage to India*, London: Penguin Classics, 2005 p.139.

Five
Psalms, hymns and not so spiritual songs

Introduction

In 1984, the *Daily Telegraph* ran an article about the different types of music that were played at crematoria during a funeral service, noting that the crematorium superintendent and funeral officiant would act as the ultimate arbiter of taste to determine whether unusual pieces of music were considered suitable or not. It reported one instance of 'Bridge over troubled waters' being under discussion, but ultimately it was deemed that this particular song was not suitable. A study two years later in 1986 reported instances of clergy walking out of funerals or demanding apologies from funeral directors because the family included a pop song in the order of service, or even because the deceased's grandchildren played the recorder as part of the service.[31]

It is hard to imagine a situation today where a Simon and Garfunkel ballad would be considered unusual, or indeed unsuitable, for a funeral – and if clergy walked out of funerals every time a pop song was played, they would rarely complete a whole service! Much has changed in the last 30 years.

However, there is a dilemma for clergy, which was hinted at in Chapter 1. Most ministers will allow secular music to be played at the beginning and end of services – but is there a line in the sand beyond which we should not go? If we allow music at the beginning and the end, is there a reason why we do not allow it in the middle of a service? If, for example, ministers felt that Frank Sinatra's 'My way' said something completely at odds with the Christian gospel, should they allow it to be played? Is it acceptable to have such pieces of music in a crematorium chapel when a minister is officiating, but not in a church? Is there a different rule for popular music than for classical pieces which can more easily be played on the organ, whether or not the latter pieces were originally composed with a church worship setting in mind? All these issues will be considered as part of this chapter.

At the heart of this dilemma is the central question of what the funeral is for. If it is only carried out to proclaim the hope of resurrection as we understand it within the Christian story, then songs and music that do not emphasise this could easily be seen as undermining it. If

---

31. See Maura Page's research reported in 'Grave Misgivings' in *Religion Today* 3: 1986 pp.7-9.

one of the stated purposes of the funeral, however, is to give thanks for the life of the deceased, then music that calls that person to mind may be seen as legitimate. Music is tremendously evocative of memories, and this chapter will consider how it can best be used within a funeral.

Of course, we are not just looking at secular pieces of music. Families are still content to sing hymns in a funeral service and would expect to do so if a Christian minister is conducting the service. When thinking about songs, neither should we forget the Psalms, which we considered in the last chapter. They are the songs in the original hymn book for followers of God, and generations will point to their words as providing succour and aid in a time of loss.

Hymns new and old

Often the experience of those attending humanist funerals or those conducted by civil celebrants is that they miss singing hymns. Given how few hymns are still known by much of society today, this may seem curious, and yet singing at a funeral is often an opportunity to allow grief to be expressed: there is safety in weeping that is not heard above the sound of singing. People welcome the opportunity to sing a hymn – they may only remember 'All things bright and beautiful' or 'The Lord's my shepherd' from their childhood, but it is important to them to sing them at a funeral.

Perhaps this underlines an important truth about funerals, which can be missed in the anxiety to make them individual and unique to each person: sometimes it is the familiar which brings the greatest comfort. Thomas Long maintains that what is needed in a Christian funeral is to do the same thing over and over because 'it is important for our bodies to know their way home'.[32] In other words, use the old familiar language, sing the hymns that were known from childhood, and do not try to create something unique every time. It is a philosophy that is at odds with much of modern funeral practice, where the key is to 'do it my way', yet there is wisdom in it.

Some hymns are more appropriate than others for a funeral, yet with many bereaved families it may not be possible to get beyond the question, 'Which hymns do you know?' The familiarity of the hymns – and perhaps the association they hold with childhood – may assist with the grieving process, so it need not be an overriding cause of concern that the words of 'All things bright and beautiful' seem so inappropriate for a funeral. Similarly, when the chief choice is 'Jerusalem', clergy often sigh and wonder whether this even qualifies as a hymn.

---

32. Long, *Accompany them with Singing*, p.19.

While there is indeed a dilemma over this hymn choice that has to be faced, it is also true that if a family is simply told that they cannot sing a particular hymn, it is likely that that will be all they remember from the service. The 'Yes' of God's grace and mercy which we proclaim in the service is replaced by the 'No' of the vicar who wouldn't let them sing 'Jerusalem'!

Yet we need not despise the paucity of choice or limits of people's hymn knowledge: other familiar hymns offer words that can provide greater meaning. 'Morning has broken' may again seem like an unpromising choice, yet it can be understood in the light of the new resurrection dawn that we know at death.

For those who are familiar with a wide range of hymns, there are a number of categories of hymns which I wish to consider. Often families will say that they do not want to sing anything too gloomy, and there are undoubtedly wonderful hymns of praise which can lift the focus of a funeral and remind everyone of the hope that is at the heart of what we do. However, sad songs should not be dismissed out of hand: if one of the purposes of a funeral is to aid the grieving process, we should not be frightened of hymns that help us do that.

One obvious group of hymns are metrical psalms, which we considered in the previous chapter – they should also be borne in mind when choosing hymns.

1. Evening hymns/hymns about death

There are a number of hymns which ostensibly are set for evening worship, yet can be read as a metaphor for death. The most common of these that are sung at funerals are 'The day thou gavest' and 'Abide with me'. It is worth spending some time looking at the latter hymn and the theology and meaning of the words.

'Abide with me' has two main connotations for people in this country: funerals and the FA Cup final. It has also been sung at the final of every Rugby League Challenge Cup since 1929, and even made an appearance at the Opening Ceremony of the London 2012 Olympic Games. Generally, people will be content to sing this hymn at a funeral because it is known from the football! Nonetheless, there are some who choose to avoid this hymn because it is seen as gloomy, with a fairly downbeat tune, 'Eventide'. It was written by Henry Francis Lyte, a Victorian hymn writer, as an evening hymn, with deliberate overtones of the ending of the metaphorical day of life. By verse two, it is clear that Lyte has this in mind, with its opening line of 'Swift to its close ebbs out life's little day'. Lyte was dying with tuberculosis when he wrote the hymn and only survived a few weeks after completing it in 1847.

What is remarkable about this hymn when compared to much modern hymn writing is that it is prepared to confront the issue of death. Many accuse the Victorians of having been obsessed with death; they had elaborate mourning rituals and spent vast sums on memorials to loved ones. It is certainly true that death was not the taboo that it became in the twentieth century. However, with such high infant mortality rates in Victorian times, that is not surprising: death was an everyday reality for most people. By the end of the twentieth century, we had hidden death away in hospitals and left it to be dealt with by professional doctors and funeral directors rather than observing it at home. In consequence, very few hymn writers, or writers of modern worship songs, are prepared to confront the issue of death in their hymns. There are notable exceptions, such as John Bell and Graham Maule from the Iona Community who have written ballads such as 'From the falter of breath', set to the traditional Scottish folk tune, 'The Iona Boat Song', but they are few.

Lyte's personal circumstances meant that he had to confront the issue of death, but he has left us with a hymn that provides a full theology of death and dying. God is sought 'through cloud and sunshine' and in the midst of change and decay. This offers a realism to life's journey, where we encounter pain. The hymn contains a declaration of faith which states that, 'I fear no foe with thee at hand to bless; ills have no weight and tears no bitterness'. For many of us, this may feel like a declaration of hoped-for faith rather than lived reality, and yet it is a declaration to which Christians can assent and should aspire – it echoes the psalmist's acknowledgement that 'though I walk through the darkest valley, I fear no evil' (Psalm 23:4). Indeed, there are many pastors who could point to examples of members of their congregations knowing this certainty – as it seems Lyte did – as their lives draw to a close.

At the heart of this hymn is St Paul's declaration from 1 Corinthians 15:55: 'Where is death's sting? Where grave thy victory?' This is the heart of the gospel and the essence of the resurrection hope to which we point people in a Christian funeral. It is this hope that enables Lyte to conclude his hymn with the final verse of triumph:

> Hold thou thy cross before my closing eyes;
> shine through the gloom and point me to the skies;
> heaven's morning breaks, and earth's vain shadows flee,
> in life, in death, O Lord, abide with me.

'Abide with me' is a hymn that is falling from favour at funerals because it is seen as too upsetting. We see the unease that people have in marking sorrow and the desire to emphasise that the service should focus on thanksgiving, not grief. But the mournful nature of the tune is not something to be avoided: it may well aid the grieving process, which is an important part of the funeral. In considering the various key aspects of the funeral which are listed at the end of Chapter 1, it both gives expression to the grief felt and offers hope for the future for the bereaved.

Hymns that deal well with the issue of death are rare: as I said, there are few hymn writers today who are prepared to tackle this issue. Yet they offer rich resources for a funeral. 'Abide with me' has the chief advantage of being well known, as well as offering words that confront the reality of death, whilst offering hope within it.

2. Hymns of pilgrimage

There are many well-known hymns which focus on the Christian life and journey. Many of these are included at the back of the service book that is used by many crematoria and cemetery chapels: hymns such as 'Lead us, heavenly Father, lead us', 'Jesus, lover of my soul' and 'O God our help in ages past'.

What is noticeable about all these hymns is that they were all written before the beginning of the twentieth century. However, this is probably simply because they are well known rather than being because of a lack of modern worship songs and hymns that deal with the issue of our journey with God. Nonetheless, it is true to say that many songs written for use in informal worship and within the charismatic and Pentecostal churches focus far more on praise of God and the good things of life than they do with the sorrow and hardships of life's journey. We are much more likely to encounter modern worship songs that echo the sentiments of the Xhosa praise song 'We are marching in the light of God' than one that expresses the anxieties of a hymn such as 'Oft in danger, oft in woe'.

This is not to say that there is no place for songs of praise at a funeral, but as Christians we do need to be able to express the pain of parting and the fear of death, as well as the joy of future hope. I want to consider one traditional hymn and two modern ones that do this well.

'Guide me O thou great Redeemer'

This, of course, is as well known as any hymn sung today – again, not least because of its sporting connections! It was written by William Williams, a Welsh hymn writer, in 1762, though the tune with which it is universally linked, *Cwm Rhondda*, was not written until 1905. It is one of the few hymns from the great Welsh hymn-singing tradition that has translated into most English hymn books. If families want a hymn that is 'a good sing' and will lift them at a funeral rather than be too mournful, they need look no further. However, the words of the hymn have real depth and express much of the crisis that is felt in life as well as its joys.

The first verse acknowledges the reality of the world around us – that, spiritually speaking, we live in a barren land. This need not be seen as a reference to the godlessness or otherwise of our society in modern Britain; rather it is simply an acknowledgement that our world is broken and is not as God intended. Central to the hope that we have as Christians is that we are moving to a new heaven and a new earth, as St John describes in Revelation 21, and all the brokenness of life will be restored to wholeness.

Williams uses imagery from the story of the Exodus to give power to his hymn. The reference to God opening the crystal fountain in verse 2 picks up the story of Moses striking the rock, told in Exodus 17 and Numbers 20, when the Israelites complain about their lack of water. In using the Exodus story, Williams follows the frequent example of the psalmist – throughout the Psalms are references to what God did in bringing the people of Israel out of Egypt and leading them to the Promised Land.

For Williams, the Promised Land is life beyond the grave, and in verse 3 he contemplates its arrival. What is most powerful about Williams' hymn is the realism with which he faces this prospect. There are many Christians today who are not prepared to acknowledge that 'when they tread the verge of Jordan', there will be anxious fears. It can seem that modern hymn writing assumes a triumphalism that does not permit any doubt, yet the reality for most of us is that the process of dying does bring fear, however strong our faith and hope is in the life beyond the grave. This hymn provides such strong resources in the face of death because it is prepared to acknowledge the fear that accompanies our journey towards the end of our life.

'Blessed be your name'

A complete contrast to this first hymn can be found in the modern worship song 'Blessed be your name', written by Matt and Beth Redman. It is a powerful example of a song that is prepared to consider the hard times of life as well as the times of joy. Redman is one of the foremost British worship leaders of this generation and his songs are sung in many churches.

Although the song starts with an affirmation of blessing of God – 'Blessed be your name in the land that is plentiful' – it is distinctive in how it continues from many modern praise songs that speak only of positive aspects of the Christian journey. The second half of the verse contrasts the opening situation by affirming that 'blessed be your name when I'm found in the desert place, though I walk through the wilderness.' The second verse similarly speaks of the time when the road is marked with suffering and there is pain in the offering. The chorus declares that even 'when the darkness closes in, Lord, still I will say, Blessed be the name of the Lord.'

There is a bridge section leading back into the chorus which declares:

You give and take away, you give and take away.
My heart will choose to say 'Lord, blessed be your name.'

Redman picks up on the words of Job 1:21 here where Job declares 'The Lord gave, and the Lord has taken away; blessed be the name of the Lord.' The words are spoken, of course, by Job in the context of the death of all his children and the destruction of his property. This verse is also one of the opening sentences spoken in the Church of England funeral service.

The pastoral strength of this song is its ability to confront the reality of life as it is experienced by people, whether they are of a strong faith or not. At the time of a funeral, there can be a sense of bewilderment that disaster has struck, and people wonder where God is in the midst of it all. To declare the name of God to be blessed in the midst of disaster goes beyond Henry Lyte's prayer that God would abide with him through cloud and sunshine – and indeed it may be more than those of little expressed faith would be prepared to say – yet for people of faith, it offers words that recognise reality and still find a way to praise God in the midst of it.

'One more step along the world'

Legend has it that Sydney Carter, the author of this song, was asked to write it in order to explain something of the process of death to children. It is a relatively recent hymn, having been written in 1971, but is very different in style from Matt Redman's song. Like most of the hymns referred to here, it is likely to be well known because it was sung in primary schools by generations of children. It may well be seen as a more suitable hymn for a wedding than a funeral, yet its words do seem apposite to those who are experiencing death and bereavement. The chorus speaks of travelling from the old to the new, with a prayer that the singer would keep travelling with God (although God is never explicitly mentioned in the hymn).

One of the strengths of this hymn lies in the upbeat tune, so families who react strongly against anything too mournful have the opportunity to sing what is perceived as a cheerful song, although it is one that provides words which the officiating minister can reflect upon and offer interpretation to the mourners.

3. Hymns of praise

The trend towards 'services of thanksgiving' rather than funerals has been accompanied by a desire to sing hymns that reflect a more cheerful mood. There are many aspects of this which should trouble us: a funeral is a time to mourn as much as it is a time to give thanks. Civil celebrants and humanist ministers focus chiefly on thanksgiving for the life of the person who has died – though it is legitimate to ask who is being thanked in a humanist service! Christian ministers have a very clear answer to this question, but we should not forget that a funeral is also a time to mourn and allow expression for grief.

Nonetheless, when it comes to hymns of thanksgiving, there is a wonderful choice. This is one area of church life where the modern worship movement has provided strength in depth of resources – so many worship and praise songs have been written in the last 30 years or so. Of course, unless the bereaved family are committed churchgoers from a tradition where these songs are sung, they will be unlikely to know many of them, so I have restricted my examples to more widely known hymns.

When planning a funeral service, it is important to take account of the shape of the service and the movement within it. Whilst I have stressed the importance of grief and mourning within the service, it may well be that by the time you reach the end of the service and the deceased has been commended to God, the focus should be on praise and trust in the hope of eternal life. Some of the most moving moments of my ministry have come at the end of a funeral service for a church member, where we have stood and sung praise to God with a hymn such as 'How great thou art'. The final verse, when we acknowledge that 'Christ shall come with shouts of acclamation, and take me home, what joy shall fill my heart', speak eloquently of the hope that we have. The loved one who has died has indeed gone home.

There are so many fine hymns to choose from that I want to mention only a few by name, rather than analysing further the text of any of them. 'Thine be the glory' reminds us that at the heart of every funeral is the hope that comes because of the death and resurrection of Christ. 'Now thank we all our God' may feel more suitable for more formal worship where people do not want to get too emotional! I officiated in two most memorable funerals where we finished with the 'Battle Hymn of the Republic'. It may have felt slightly out of place to sing this in very British, formal Anglican worship, yet its opening line of 'Mine eyes have seen the glory of the coming of the Lord' spoke powerfully of the reality which we believed that the deceased Christian now knew.

The limited selection of hymns chosen for funerals can seem sad. So many wonderful words have been written, it can feel frustrating to sing the same few hymns over and over again. However, as I said, there is a strength in that, too – and given that this is the reality that Christian ministers know all too well, it is as well to acknowledge the strength that singing something familiar offers to the grieving process. However, if the families are able to be more adventurous in their choices, the hymn singing offers the opportunity to allow expression of grief and something of the journey of grief, and also to end on a note of thanksgiving and praise for the hope that is present thanks to the death and resurrection of Christ.

Other music

It is this aspect of music at funerals which is most difficult for most clergy and which has changed the most over the last 20 years. The reminder of Elton John singing 'Candle in the wind' for Princess Diana has acted as a spur to families in this country that they should not restrict their music to traditional hymns or other pieces ordinarily deemed suitable for a church service.

There are a number of issues to consider:

- Does it make a difference as to whether the main part of the service is held in church or in the crematorium/cemetery chapel?
- Should such music be restricted to the beginning and the end, or will it work in the middle of a service?
- What limits should be placed on the sort of music played?

Every minister conducting a funeral will have their own answer to each of these questions. All I propose to do in this section is offer some reflections on the choices made.

The first issue does seem to be the most spurious, yet I have heard of clergy colleagues who have refused to play a music CD in the church and suggested that it would sound much better at the committal service in the crematorium afterwards. Clearly, there is a practical issue of whether the church has a decent enough sound system for a CD to be heard clearly. Many churches still have simple sound systems without an integrated CD player, and a recorded piece of music would not sound particularly good when played to a congregation full of people.

If a church does not have a decent sound system, there are ways around this to play recorded music. Since the advent of MP3 players and smartphones, music can be downloaded onto these devices and played through a docking station costing less than £100 to a level that could fill a small church. Indeed, if there is a sound system, the most effective way to play the music may be to put the piece on an MP3 player and play it via a lead through the sound system rather than burning a CD separately.

Given that a lot of smaller churches have to rely on recorded music anyway for the singing of hymns, through such collections as *No Organist? No Problem!*[33], there can be no justification to refuse to play CDs on principle in church. Clearly there may be an issue around what the piece of music is, and that will be considered below.

At most funerals conducted by a church minister, non-religious pieces of music tend to be restricted to the beginning and end of the service as the coffin is brought in and as the people leave. However, there are difficulties with this. Often, as the coffin is being brought in, the minister is reading sentences of Scripture to mark the beginning of the service. If the piece of music is longer than two minutes or so, it will need to be brought to an abrupt halt halfway through, or everybody stands in silence waiting for the piece to finish and uncertain what to do. An opposite problem occurs when the music is at the end: if it is a long piece, most of the congregation are long gone while the music is just getting going, or everyone stands in their places and does not move until it is finished. The last scenario can be satisfactory if the minister has made it clear that this is what is going to happen, but it can lead to uncertainty.

It is certainly worth considering whether a piece of music could be placed in the middle of the service. It can provide a pause for everyone in the congregation to call upon their own reflections and memories of the person who has died. If it is a piece of music that was strongly associated with the deceased, its very playing will call him or her to mind in a helpful way. Some funerals can seem filled with spoken words, and to provide some respite from this with a song or other musical piece can help with the pace of the funeral and offer a moment of peace and reflection. It seems entirely natural to do this when there is a live singer or musician to perform the piece, but somehow we are less comfortable when the music is recorded. I am aware that many of my colleagues would disagree with me on this and feel that a pop song in the middle of a service is somehow not fitting.

This leads us to the third question: are there types of music that are not fitting for a church service or for a funeral? Often the family will have an instinctive sense of what they feel to be appropriate in a church, and there is little point seeking to undermine them in that. However, I do not believe it is possible to offer hard and fast rules beyond basic rules of decency and legality.

I think the most dangerous instinct in this is to imagine that it is all right to play classical music on an organ but not contemporary music through a sound system. One of the most popular pieces of music to

---

33. A CD collection of popular hymns produced by Kevin Mayhew to assist churches that have no regular organist or musicians.

play at a wedding is the Bridal March by Wagner – a man who inspired Adolf Hitler! However, few vicars consider that it is completely unsuitable for a wedding for this reason. We ought to be similarly cautious about banning music at a funeral simply because it was not originally written with a religious context in mind.

We acknowledge that one of the purposes of a funeral is to give thanks for a person. We do that by calling them to mind, and music helps us to do that. It may well be that their musical choices will not match our own, but if a particular song helps the mourners remember the person, we can assist in the mourning process by making sure it can be played. At the funeral of a 16-year-old boy who was a fan of thrash metal music, we played one of his favourite tracks in the middle of the service. For most of the congregation the music was fairly incomprehensible, but they could not listen to it without thinking of David and the times he had played it when they were with him.

At a funeral I conducted for a 23-year-old Liverpool fan who had died suddenly from a brain haemorrhage, we played 'You'll never walk alone' in the middle of the service, and the whole congregation, many wearing Liverpool scarves, rose as one to stand in silence or to join in with the singing. What made that service even more extraordinary and poignant was that the young man had died on the anniversary of the Hillsborough stadium disaster. In standing and listening to that piece of music, inextricably linked in this country with Liverpool FC, we remembered not just Graeme but also those fans who had been killed some 15 years previously. The playing of that anthem was an integral part of the whole service, and not simply something that should have been played while going out or coming into church, or just at the crematorium.

In 2009, The Co-operative Funeralcare carried out a survey of the ten most popular contemporary pieces of music to be played in funerals. The list reads as follows:

1. 'My way' by Frank Sinatra or Shirley Bassey
2. 'Wind beneath my wings' by Bette Midler or Celine Dion
3. 'Time to say goodbye' by Andrea Boccelli and Sarah Brightman
4. 'Angels' by Robbie Williams
5. 'Somewhere over the rainbow' by Eva Cassidy
6. 'You raise me up' by Boyzone, Westlife or Josh Grobin
7. 'My heart will go on' by Celine Dion
8. 'I will always love you' by Witney Houston
9. 'You'll never walk alone' by Gerry and the Pacemakers
10. 'Unforgettable' by Nat King Cole

Most of these choices seem entirely uncontentious. Some even offer words that speak to the human longing for a different and better world, such as 'Somewhere over the rainbow'. The themes of leave-taking and loss pervade 'Time to say goodbye', and the thanksgiving for the life of another offered in 'You raise me up' or 'Wind beneath my wings' seem very fitting in thanksgiving for the life of another.

And then there is 'My way'! The words of this song are those of someone looking back on their life as it draws to a close and celebrating the fact that they lived their life as they wanted to. The irony of families choosing this piece of music is that they will often go on to tell you that their loved one lived for their family and did all they could for them – in other words, the selfishness that seems to pervade the words of the song were not lived out in the life of this particular individual. Perhaps it is possible to read the words of the song as indicating someone who had the courage to make their own choices, and that sometimes those choices were to serve others. Personally, I think that is being too generous to its sentiments, and I suspect that a life lived with regrets too few to mention is a life lived refusing to face up to the times when we got it wrong and failed others. I also think the song offers a strong contrast to Jesus' words from John 14:6, where he says, 'I am the way, and the truth, and the life.' Perhaps it is incumbent on those who minister at funerals to point out the paucity of the philosophy of life that 'My way' inhabits. Rather than ban it altogether, we would do better to show the family that the evidence of the deceased appears to show that they did not simply live according to this mantra, and the love that they showed for their family offered a different, less selfish philosophy.

On a number of occasions in Scripture, St Paul takes the philosophy of the surrounding culture and uses it to illustrate a gospel truth. Remember his sermon in Acts 17 in Athens at the Areopagus where, in verse 28, he quotes a contemporary poet who wrote that 'we too are his [i.e. God's] offspring.' Similarly, in the letter to Titus, a disparaging reference is given to Cretans from one of their own writers who describes them as 'always liars, vicious brutes, lazy gluttons'(Titus 1:12).

William Booth, the founder of the Salvation Army, is said to have asked the question, 'Why should the devil have all the best tunes?' and used many of those tunes as the setting for Christian hymns. We also should not be afraid to listen to those tunes and allow them to speak to us. In the context of a funeral, they will remind us of the person who has died and enable us to give thanks for them as well as to mourn. It is then the role of the minister to remind the congregation of the hope that we can have in the midst of our grief.

Six
The symbols of death and life

> The family is seated. The flowers are beautiful. The seats in the chapel are full of friends and acquaintances. The prelude music fades out. And then something amazing happens.
>
> The officiant stands up and takes everyone in attendance on a journey of the deceased's life . . . At the end of the service, each person in attendance is handed a piece from a Scrabble game because this lady loved to play Scrabble. They are invited to put that tile in a special place in order to remember her life in the coming days.
>
> To close the service, everyone stands and sings 'The Fishy Song' together.
>
> The family is thrilled that their loved one was given such a special and sacred time of remembrance. The attendees hug the family and tell them that they were so glad they came.[34]

A scrabble piece may well be a more unusual symbol to be associated with a funeral. Indeed, the tone of the website suggests that it is precisely because it is so unusual that it should be celebrated. There is a suggestion in the writing that this funeral is special, because it has been able to make use of symbols as well as words and music.

Symbols do not simply stand on their own: they represent something. A scrabble piece on its own is meaningless and useless – it can do little more than be left in a pocket or bag before being thrown out when discovered. But as an object that has power to evoke memory, it is a symbol – in this case, of a loved woman, perhaps a mother, a wife, a sister, a friend.

All funerals are full of symbolic meaning, and symbols vie with each other throughout the service. It is not simply now that people choose to release a dove or balloons after the service, or place a military sword or emblem on the coffin as it is carried in: the very choice of cremation or burial is heavy with symbolic meaning.

The Christian faith has recognised from the first the power of symbols. The sacraments are symbols of our faith – outward signs of inward grace, as they have been defined. We should therefore be accustomed to recognising them when we see them and be attuned to interpreting them. However, what seems to be very sad about many funerals conducted by Christian ministers is that we have flattened them out and removed so much of the symbolism – or worse, that

---

34. From the website of County Celebrants Network – see http://www.countycelebrantsnetwork.biz/A-Civil-Funeral-Ceremony.html (accessed 23 April 2013).

where there are obvious symbols for interpretation, we have refused to do so, or to consider their significance.

I am sure that one of the reasons why services conducted by civil celebrants have become so popular today is that they allow the power of symbols to speak. When a dove is released at the end of a cremation or burial service, people understand the symbolism of a spirit set free to soar into the sky. It is no good to respond that this shows a shaky understanding of life after death, or that it represents an unhelpful body–spirit dualism that has little to do with orthodox Christian faith. The symbol is interpreted by the mourners in a way which accords with what they have been taught from their youngest days about death – namely, that we leave our bodies behind and our spirits go 'up' into heaven to be with God. It is also becoming a popular practice to release a helium balloon at a funeral – particularly when there are young children amongst the mourners, or the person who has died is a child – and the same symbolism is at work here.

As Christian ministers, it is not hard to point out the links between such symbolism and the Christian story – the Holy Spirit as a dove and Christ's ascension into heaven are the two most obvious parallels. It is possible, therefore, to build on the symbols offered in a modern funeral service and point the way to Christ and his love for the one who has died and the mourners in their grief.

There is not space in any book to consider all the various symbols that crop up in funerals. Some, like the scrabble pieces in the opening story, are individual and unique to the person who has died: others, such as doves and balloons, are becoming more popular. In this chapter, I want to consider three symbolic worlds and the symbols attached to them from a Christian perspective. The first of these, most fundamentally, is the symbolism of burial and cremation. The shift, in this country at least, from burial to cremation, has happened over the last 100 years, but recently there has been some resistance to cremation, with the rise of natural burial grounds.

Secondly, I wish to consider some of the symbolism that arises from the understanding of the Christian life as a pilgrimage from cradle to grave. When we see the funeral in the light of this pilgrimage, the journey that the coffin makes takes on particular significance: it is not simply about getting the coffin from one place to another; the actual journey has significance. How is that journey marked, and how does it link into the Christian pilgrimage which begins at our baptism and is transformed at our death into a journey with One whom we see face to face, rather than in a glass darkly?

The third symbol that I wish to consider in this chapter is the central sacrament of our faith, Holy Communion. In that sacrament, we remember the death of Christ. If a funeral is, as Paul Sheppy maintains, a re-enactment of the Easter event, it seems appropriate that Communion should be central to a funeral conducted by a Christian minister. However, it seems that it is only in the Roman Catholic Church that the Mass is routinely observed in a funeral. What can we learn from that tradition about its power at the time of death?

Cremation versus burial

The first cremation in modern Britain took place in 1884, when Dr William Price of Llantrisant, Wales, cremated the body of his young son. Price was an eccentric man who claimed to be the archdruid of a lost Celtic tribe, and he named his son Jesus Christ. The boy had died aged only five months, and Price was prosecuted for disposing of his body by an illegal means. When he was found 'not guilty', the gates were effectively opened for cremation to take place in this country. In the following year, three more people were cremated, and this figure had risen to 444 by 1900. Around the turn of the century, both Hull and Golders Green in North London opened crematoria. As we saw in Chapter 1, most people in this country are now cremated on their death, and the figures for cremation have been fairly constant for the last 25 years.[35]

Through the twentieth century, the Church all over the world had to grapple with its response to cremation. Unsurprisingly, different denominations reached different conclusions. The Eastern Orthodox Churches have been most steadfast in their opposition to cremation, though in the era of the Soviet Union, when many cemeteries fell into a state of disrepair, it seemed as though the Russian Orthodox Church acquiesced to an increased use of cremation. In Greece, it is traditional for the bodies of the dead to be exhumed a few years after death and the bones placed in an ossuary, provided the flesh has all decayed. This exhumation is an important part of Greek life and identity, so there has not been any significant take-up of cremation in that country.

In this country, as we have seen, the Church of England decided between 1937 and 1944 in a series of debates that there was 'no theological significance' behind the practice of cremation, so its ministers were able to preside at cremations, and suitable liturgy was provided. The heart of the decision in the debates rested on the undoubted truth that God was just as able to raise resurrection bodies from ashes as he was

---

35. It is interesting and significant in the history of funerals that a similar battle to Dr Price's has been fought in recent years by a Hindu, Davender Ghai, who won a High Court battle in 2010 for his body to be disposed of in the traditional Hindu method of an outdoor pyre. His case has been championed by the Natural Death Centre, and although there are many more legal hurdles to jump, it seems as though other traditional methods of body disposal will be allowed.

from decaying corpses, so cremation would not do anything that would cause a problem for God.

This, of course, is true. If God created humanity from the dust of the earth, he is surely able to create a new humanity from ashes. However, the problem is not with the theological significance of cremation, but its symbolic significance. What is the symbolism attached to burning a body to ash, as opposed to placing it in the ground?

In the first English Prayer Book of 1549, the minister said a collect, which included the following lines:

> O Merciful God . . . who hath taught us by his holy apostle Paul not to be sorry as men without hope for them that sleep in him: we meekly beseech thee, O Father, to raise us from the death of sin, unto the life of righteousness, that *when we shall depart this life, we may sleep in him, as our hope is this our brother/sister doeth, and at the general resurrection in the last day, both we and this our brother/sister departed, receiving again our bodies, and rising again in thy most gracious favour, may with all thine elect saints, obtain eternal joy.* (My emphasis)

A clear symbolic world is painted here. The dead are placed in their graves in order to sleep and wait for the general resurrection on the last day. At that time, they – and we when we are dead – will receive new resurrection bodies as part of the new redeemed humanity. This accords well with the Apostles' Creed, where we declare, 'I believe in the Resurrection of the Body'.

Think of the painting by Sir Stanley Spencer, *The Resurrection, Cookham*. This captures exactly the worldview expressed by this collect. In the painting, the dead are coming out of their graves in new bodies in order to rise again at the last day. That was the hope as understood by Christians for many centuries – and for this reason, St Paul says in 1 Thessalonians 4:16, 'the dead in Christ will rise first'. They will then be joined by those who are still alive at the time of the general resurrection.

Now consider the symbolism of cremation. At the heart of this ceremony is the perception that the body doesn't matter: what is important is the soul, so it is all right for the body to be burnt because it is simply a shell. The soul has already left the body and can be united with God. This is not specifically said at any point in a Christian funeral service at the crematorium, but as people understand the significance of cremation it is hard not to draw this conclusion.

Why does this matter? Some would say that the medieval view of death and what happens to our bodies is extremely naive and will bear little resemblance to what actually happens. Many people believe that we are united with God at the point of death, not at some indeterminate point in the future. Most Christians, indeed, speak of loved ones who have died as already with God, not as waiting for the general resurrection. They may be right insofar as eternity is outside this world's realm of time, so it is possible to speak of things having happened in eternity which in this world we consider to be taking place in the future.

I believe that a preference for burial over cremation accords better with the symbolism that is linked to the resurrection of the body rather than the immortality of the soul. However, I am aware that many Christians believe that the immortality of the soul represents a better understanding of how we will be after death. Indeed, some official Church teaching has leant in this direction. What is ironic about the Church of England decisions is that they were made at the time when William Temple was the Archbishop of Canterbury, and he was quite clear that the true Christian notion of our lives after death was with the resurrection of the body. This is what happened to Jesus after his resurrection, so in some way it will happen to us. In a lecture he gave in 1932, he wrote:

> Man is not immortal by nature or right; but he is capable of immortality and there is offered to him resurrection from the dead and life eternal if he will receive it from God and on God's terms.[36]

However, given the prevalence of cremation in this country – and, indeed, its ever-increasing use in much of the world – we should consider how its symbols should be used within the service. One of the difficulties for the symbolic world it paints is that its central symbol is hidden. When a person is buried, everyone stands round the coffin and watches it being lowered into the ground. With cremation, all that is seen in many crematoria nowadays is a curtain that is drawn around the coffin. We all know that the coffin is sent off to be placed in the cremators, but we do not see that take place. (It is interesting to note

---

36. William Temple, *Nature, Man & God*, Edinburgh: T & T Clark, 1934, p.472.

that people have a right to watch the coffin go in to the cremator, but most do not exercise that option. However, for some faiths, such as Hinduism, there is an expectation that the family will watch this. In areas of this country where there is a high proportion of Hindu funerals, some crematoria have created special areas where families can watch the cremation.)

The central symbol of cremation is, of course, fire – and that is part of the problem for Christians. In some old crematoria, at the end of the service the coffin descended to a lower level before being taken off for the cremation process. Many families found this extremely upsetting – and yet, a coffin is similarly lowered at a burial. Somehow, the association with fire, rather than earth, made the lowering of a coffin feel as though the body was going down to hell. Although there are positive connections with fire in the Christian faith – think of the Holy Spirit descending at Pentecost – there are also many negative ones.

This seems to emphasise the central difficulty that the Church of England did not fully address in its debates. The problems with cremation are not with theology, but with symbolism. It did nothing to address these problems – and few other denominations did either. Although the symbolism of cremation is very different from that of burial, the service offered is no different. There are very few liturgies offered that pick up on the symbolism of fire and incorporate them into the service, beyond the reference to 'ashes to ashes, dust to dust' which the minister speaks at the time of the committal. Professor Douglas Davies of the Centre for Death and Life Studies at the University of Durham has written one possibility which picks up on the symbolism:

> As the flames of earth consume our mortality,
> so in the fullness of time the flame of your love
> may remake us eternally in the glory and stature of Christ,
> who alone is the Light of the World,
> the light that no darkness can end,
> who with you and the Holy Spirit
> is God for ever and ever. Amen.[37]

This prayer reminds us of the possible links between fire and light – links, of course, that are often made through the lighting of a candle flame in church.

The other problem that is also not addressed with cremation is that the act of cremation is not the final disposal of the body: there are then ashes which must be dealt with. It is, of course, possible to inter ashes, or to scatter them, but very little ritual is offered for this. Indeed, often the interment of ashes takes place long after the funeral – sometimes several years later. Furthermore, some people find themselves unable

---

37. Douglas Davies, *The Theology of Death*, London: T & T Clark, 2008, p.145.

to take this final step, and their loved one's ashes remain in the house – on the mantelpiece, in the bathroom cabinet, tucked away in a wardrobe. They are placed there, not because that is to be their final resting place, but because the next of kin cannot summon the strength to complete the process, and it seems as though there is not much help to do it.

I think we should be under no doubt that cremation is here to stay. Although I have expressed unease at the symbolism that it offers, it does not necessarily follow that we should maintain that it is incompatible with a Christian view of the disposal of the body. However, I think the Church should offer better explanations of the symbolism of cremation and provide liturgy that helps us make sense of what is happening.

Natural burial: The rise of the alternative ceremony

The first natural burial ground in Britain was opened in Carlisle in 1993. Less than 20 years later, there are over 200 such grounds listed, though often they are no more than a section of a municipal cemetery. Burials that take place at such places are often referred to as 'woodland burials', though often the grounds are still open fields in which trees are being planted to represent each burial that takes place there. More than half of the sites are run by the local authority, and many are part of an existing cemetery. The remainder are privately managed. In 1994, the Association of Natural Burial Grounds (ANBG) was established by the Natural Death Centre, and a number of natural burial grounds belong to the ANBG. With the rise of ecological awareness in Britain, and a desire to seek environmentally friendly solutions to many aspects of life and death, there has been a sharp increase in the use of natural burial grounds. Indeed, there are more natural burial grounds in this country than crematoria, although far fewer ceremonies are performed there.

Like cremation, there is little formal liturgy written specially for natural burials. In 2002, the Diocese of Ely opened the Arbory Trust, which describes itself on its website as 'the first Christian woodland burial charity',[38] but a distinctively Christian presence seems otherwise absent from the world of natural burials. Douglas Davies points out the symbolism of the dust of death becoming the dust of life as trees are planted alongside and nourished by the decaying corpse. Further, the oft-used description of the cross as the tree on which Jesus hung and that tree of judgement thereby becoming the tree of hope and life also offers strong links for theologians and liturgists to make.[39]

---

38. See www.arborytrust.org (accessed 23 April 2013).
39. See Davies, *Theology*, p.118.

The natural associations that woodland burials make – with our bodies decomposing and thereby nourishing the soil to which they have returned – offer strong resonances with people. Sceptics point out that if our bodies really were to have a beneficial effect on the ground, they should be buried in shallow graves, much closer to the surface, rather than at depth – but it is clear that, at a symbolic level, natural burial has power to connect with a worldview where, in death, we return to nature and nourish it, just as we were nourished by it in life.

The Christian pilgrimage from cradle to grave

When a person has lived in the same town all his or her life, sometimes at their death the family will ask the undertakers to take them on a journey from the house to the church or crematorium via the various homes that the person lived in through their life, or past other places in the town which had significance for them through their life. This seems to me to be an important statement about life's journey. At our funerals, it is not simply that we speak of the person's life: the journey of that person's life is, in a small way, re-enacted on the way to the funeral service.

The religious word for understanding life's journey is 'pilgrimage'. It is not a specifically Christian word, but it has important resonances for the Christian. For the last 2000 years, people have recognised special places of pilgrimage, such as Jerusalem, Rome, Santiago di Compostela and Iona. All of these places take on significance because of the journey that needs to be made in order to get there. For Christians, the roots of pilgrimage go back into our Jewish heritage: we know that Jesus went on pilgrimages regularly from the age of 12 throughout his life up to Jerusalem to observe the religious festivals such as the Passover. The Songs of Ascents in the Psalms – Psalms 120 to 134 – were traditionally sung by pilgrims on their way to Jerusalem.

It is not simply that as Christians we recognise special places of pilgrimage: our whole life's journey can be seen as a pilgrimage towards God. That is why books such as *Pilgrim's Progress* take such a hold on the religious imagination, and why hymns of pilgrimage – such as 'Guide me O thou great Redeemer', or even 'O when the saints go marching in' – are such favourites: they resonate with our notions of life as a journey.

How does this affect the way we view a funeral?

I think that firstly, it is rather undermined when the disposal of a person's body takes place away from the funeral and the coffin is not present. Of course, there will be times when it is not possible to have the body at the service – perhaps because the body has been lost and could not be recovered, or donated to medical science – but it is sad that it is becoming increasingly the norm, rather than the exception, that the body is disposed of before the main service.

Thomas Long expresses this most eloquently:

> The Christian dead should be welcomed once again to their own funerals. If they cannot literally be there in bodily presence, then we must summon every gift of language we have to establish their embodied presence in our memories and imaginations. How else are we going to experience the blessed burden of carrying them to the waiting arms of God, singing as we go?[40]

He says that the funeral is not there just to comfort the bereaved, but to tell the Christian story. In telling the Christian story, we speak of the pilgrimage that we make from cradle to grave. There are a number of symbolic ways we can do this.

Nowadays, it is usual for the coffin to be brought in by professional pall-bearers provided by the funeral directors, but there are still many occasions when the family bring their loved one into the church or chapel. I think that when this happens, it underlines the journey that is being made. Where a much-loved father or mother is carried in by his or her children and grandchildren, it speaks eloquently of the loving care that was given by that person to their children in their life: in their lifetime, they carried their children, and now, in death, their children carry them.

In some church traditions, the body is clothed in a white shroud to resemble the clothes of baptism, and on occasion, the coffin is sprinkled with water. This is done as a reminder of baptism: at the end of the earthly Christian journey, symbolism from its start is emphasised. It seems particularly appropriate to do this at the church door – just as in many old churches the font is near the church door. Thus the entrance into the Christian life is marked at the entrance to the church. If a funeral is a retelling of the Christian story in the life of this person, it seems appropriate to remember their baptism at the start of the service.

In this country, it is most common for close family and friends only to walk into the church or chapel behind the coffin: other mourners tend to be already gathered in the church. However, at a church service where the coffin has to go for its final journey to a crematorium or a cemetery, I think there is real power in inviting the whole congregation to accompany the deceased person on the final stage of their journey. In practical terms, that journey may only be as far as the church gate, or to the grave, if the burial takes place in the churchyard. However, it reinforces the sense of joining with the loved one on their journey into

---

40. Long, *Accompany them with Singing*, p.35.

God's arms and stresses that it is not 'merely a shell' in the coffin, but a person beloved of God as he or she is beloved of those who gather.

The symbolism of pilgrimage is a powerful image which can underpin a whole funeral service. Jesus speaks of an onward journey in John 14 when he says he is going to the Father to prepare a place for us: we, too, will journey on to the home of God from our funeral.

Pilgrimage is also generally a corporate activity: rarely will pilgrims make the journey alone. So, at a funeral, we should encourage the mourners to see themselves as being part of the pilgrimage with the deceased. They walked with the loved one in life, and now they accompany them for the first part of their journey to God in death. At the graveside, or at the church gate as we wave them off to the crematorium, or at the crematorium chapel when we have all gathered there, we commend them on their way to the waiting arms of God.

Holy Communion: its place at a funeral

In Roman times, when a person died, a coin was often placed in their mouth as a *viaticum* (literally 'go with me'). This was seen as payment for Charon, the ferryman of the dead, who would carry the dead over into the underworld. Early Christians followed many of the Roman practices at death, but adapted them and used them in accordance with their own beliefs. They did not just do this at death, of course – many of our Christian celebrations, including Christmas, took over the timings of ancient pagan festivals.

Early Christians adapted the practice of changing the viaticum from a coin to the bread of the Eucharist. Their hope was to die with the Eucharist still in their mouths at the time of death, so when death was delayed, it was given frequently. Finally, the Eucharistic host was placed at death as a viaticum to provide strength for the journey.

Thomas Long points out a number of moments in the early Christian rituals that had resonance with the Eucharist. As well as the viaticum, when the body reached the graveside for burial, there would be prayers and occasionally a funeral sermon. Then, in a unique gesture, the Christians would gather round the body and each give him or her the kiss of Eucharist. This is astonishing when we consider that both Jews and Greeks would have regarded such a practice with suspicion – Jews because dead bodies were considered unclean, and Greeks because they despised the physical body as a mere shell, whose soul had departed from it. Frequently, after the burial had taken place, either round the graveside or back at the home, a Eucharistic meal was then shared with Christians.[41]

---

41. Long, *Accompany them with Singing*, p.71.

Why has the Eucharist become so marginalised at funerals today? It seems strange that it was seen as such a central part of the whole symbolism of funerals in the early days, but in this country, it is only in the Roman Catholic Church that it is still routinely a part of the funeral service. It was, of course, at the heart of the Reformation controversies whether Jesus was physically or symbolically present at the Eucharist, or whether it was just a meal in memory of his death. In many Protestant churches in this country today, Communion does not form the central act of worship week by week amongst Christians, but only happens irregularly. In the Church of England, most parish churches have now restored the Eucharist to being the central act of worship week by week – and yet, even though Church of England ministers carry out the majority of funerals in this country, they still very rarely offer Communion as a standard part of that service. Of course, there are exceptions to this: in Anglican churches that describe themselves as Anglo-Catholic or 'High Church', it would be more normal. However, I believe that these are exceptions.

What is the problem here? The Communion service has been seen supremely as a service for insiders – a badge of belonging, as it were. In the Catholic Church in this country, there is still a strong sense of identity and belonging for those who are Catholic – a Catholic funeral would only be chosen where the deceased owned that sense of Catholic identity. Therefore, it is easier for Catholic priests to offer Communion as part of the funeral ritual, even if a significant number of the mourners would not be comfortable with receiving Communion.

Although many people in this country describe themselves as Church of England, they do not attach that same level of identity and belonging to that label as Catholics do: they may see themselves as Church of England, but they do not call themselves communicant members of the Church of England. Therefore, for the officiating minister at a funeral, to include Holy Communion at the service is not something which expresses the identity of the one who has died.

Even among very committed Christians, there is often a reluctance for Communion to be celebrated within the funeral service because of the awareness that many in the congregation would not be familiar or comfortable with the Communion service. I have known church members who received the Eucharist themselves two or three times a week, but would not want it at their funeral because their children did not share their beliefs. When the funeral is seen primarily as being there to offer comfort for the family rather than for the dead person, then the Eucharist might seem out of place.

However, if the funeral is for the deceased, where that person was a committed Christian, it seems strange that all symbolism of the Eucharist is removed. It is the food that nourishes us through our Christian pilgrimage, and I think the Church should think carefully about how it can be used in a funeral. Paul Sheppy is a Baptist minister, so from a tradition where the Eucharist is not such a central part of worship. However, he argues that the Church would do well to recover some of the symbolism that the viaticum brought to early funerals. Even when the Eucharist is not celebrated, he believes that the symbolism of Jesus as the bread of life should be brought into prayers and readings. This is certainly a start, but I wonder if a creative liturgist could not go beyond this in bringing the Eucharistic host into the actual service, even if Communion is not offered to everyone present.

At a funeral I conducted recently, there was an opportunity to do this. Robin and his wife had been committed members of our church for a number of years, and in the days and weeks leading up to his death, he had planned his funeral carefully. However, the family faced the modern dilemma of how to cope with the fact that if they went to the crematorium after the main funeral service, they would not get back to the wake after the cremation for at least an hour after the funeral had ended, and many of their friends with whom they wished to spend time would have left. They did not want Robin to go to the crematorium on his own: he was not 'simply a shell' to be abandoned by them as his body was committed for cremation. They were also uncomfortable about taking Robin straight to the crematorium prior to the church service: the church in our town had been his spiritual home for many years, and it seemed wrong that he would not be taken there in death.

We solved this problem by taking up a practice which, again, is more common in Roman Catholic churches than elsewhere. Robin was brought into the church the night before the funeral. At the church door, we sprinkled the coffin with water to remind us of the start of Robin's pilgrimage of faith in his baptism and placed him before the altar. We then had a small service, with about 40 family and close friends present. The central focus of this service was the Eucharist, as we commended Robin on his journey to God. The following morning, close family travelled with him to the crematorium for the committal of his body, and then about 300 people gathered in church once again for a memorial and thanksgiving service.

This was not a straightforward solution: there were a lot of church services that the immediate family had to get through! But they found great strength in the small service on eve of the funeral: it was a time for them in a building which had been Robin's spiritual home. By sharing Communion together, we were reminded of Christ's death and resurrection, which gives us hope in the face of death, and were offered spiritual strength for the journey ahead.

Conclusion

We ignore symbols at our peril. Funerals are packed full of them and it seems that many people want those symbols to speak to them. When the Church is unable to offer them, or fails to interpret them for people, they turn to their own symbolic world. Many of the symbols that people use can have real spiritual power and speak eloquently of hope after death. However, when the Church has so many good symbols and symbolic worlds of its own, it seems a shame that we do not offer them at the point of need. The life of Christian pilgrimage, sustained by the Eucharist through life, at death offers a vision of the world where death is a point in the journey. It is not simply a full stop, the end of the journey, but rather is a stepping-off point to a different stage of the journey. When viewed in this way, it can be seen that the funeral is an important ritual for the dead, not simply for the living: we send them on their way rather than simply remember them for all they did on their life's journey.

Although I personally think that burial offers a symbolic worldview that is closer to traditional Christian belief than cremation, we must accept that cremation is here to stay. Its symbolism is powerful and eloquent, so why has the Church done so little to help people understand that symbolism in a way that is compatible with traditional Christian belief? Douglas Davies' prayer, which I have quoted in this chapter, reminds us that fire can have creative powers of remaking and shaping. These are notions which could be extremely helpful in shaping a Christian liturgy of cremation. Whether we go for burial or cremation, let us find words and music that amplify the symbolism of the occasion and point to God's love and welcome at the time of death.

Seven
The funerals we all dread

Sometimes it is obvious from the first phone call. When the funeral director's opening words are, 'I have got Mr and Mrs Jones with me and they would like a minister to conduct their funeral of their baby daughter,' you know that this will be a difficult funeral. The funeral of a child always raises particular issues for us nowadays. Because infant mortality rates have plummeted so significantly, it is a much rarer event – thank God – than it was even 75 years ago, and it requires special considerations. These will be looked at in the next chapter.

However, there are a number of other funerals that also raise particular problems, and sometimes those difficulties do not reveal themselves until well into the planning for the service. What happens when it transpires from your conversations with the next of kin that their relative has committed suicide? In the depths of people's minds and understanding is the traditional belief that suicide is the unforgivable sin and therefore their loved one has gone straight to hell. Can we still offer them a Christian burial, or conduct a service at the crematorium on their behalf?

Similarly, you may find yourself conducting a service for someone who has absolutely no kin, and there is no one who can organise the funeral on their behalf. You may find that you are conducting a service where the only other person present is the funeral director – and sometimes not even they will be present.

The opposite situation can be equally difficult to deal with. There are always deaths in our society which grab the headlines – perhaps because the one who has died was brutally murdered, or was a police officer killed in the line of duty, or the person had been a famous celebrity. In these circumstances, it is likely that there will be hundreds of people at the funeral, and representatives of the media will similarly gather to record the service. What assistance can we find when doing such services?

Death by suicide: the unforgivable sin?
Colin Murray Parkes, in his work on the process of bereavement, suggests that the first response we make in the face of bereavement is shock and denial. Often we feel numb and cannot believe that the person has died. When the person has died as a result of their own action, that sense of shock is increased tenfold. There are a number

of other conflicting emotions that relatives experience following a suicide, including:

- Guilt that they did not take any action to prevent the death happening
- Confusion that they missed the signs that their relative was going to do this
- Anger with the person for taking a perceived 'easy way out'
- Relief that a person's mental or physical torment is now over.

With the increased media spotlight on the issue of assisted suicide for those facing chronic or terminal illness, this issue has become even more difficult to deal with. The Church has always taught that suicide is a sin – though nearly every mainline denomination says that it is not the unforgiveable sin – yet many in society hold that assisted suicide in certain circumstances is the humane and right thing to do. Ministering to a family where there has been a suicide following chronic illness which has required the assistance of another family member, requires real wisdom and sensitivity.

1. Suicide in Scripture

There are no direct moral commandments in Scripture forbidding suicide. However, in considering this issue, it is impossible to ignore the sixth commandment – You shall not murder (Exodus 20:13). Suicide is the deliberate taking of a life unlawfully and is in effect self-murder. However, it would be rare that there was not some element of 'diminished responsibility' due to an unbalanced mental state, and given that suicide has not been a criminal offence since 1961, it is not helpful to consider it in the light of legal categories and defences. Rather than seeing Scripture as a legal text book, we should look at the stories of suicide in the Bible and see if we can learn anything from them.

There were a number of people who committed suicide in Scripture, and what is most notable about their deaths is that no moral comment is made on the manner of them. In Judges 16, for example, we are told of the death of Samson. He killed himself by pushing over the pillars of a house in which some 3000 Philistine men and women were feasting, thereby killing them at the same time. His death is not normally regarded as suicide because his primary intent was to kill the enemy rather than himself, but he still prays to God, 'Let me die with the Philistines' (Judges 16:30). His prayer is answered, and the story is told as though this episode is the climax of Samson's ministry as a judge amongst the people of Israel.

The best-known example of suicide in the Bible is Judas Iscariot. Matthew's Gospel recounts Judas' guilt and contrition when he considers what he has done and returns the 30 pieces of silver to the chief priests and elders. In Matthew 27:5, he throws down the pieces of silver and goes out and hangs himself. It is this story of suicide that has dominated the church's response to suicide through the ages: Judas Iscariot is condemned to eternal damnation because of his betrayal of Christ, and the fact that he took his own life only adds to the guilt surrounding him. If this is the only story of suicide from the Bible that people are aware of, it is unsurprising that they will fear the Church's verdict on a loved one who acts in a similar way.

However, perhaps even the death of Judas Iscariot is not so straightforward. In the alternative account of his death in the Acts of Apostles, it is not immediately clear that this is what happened. St Luke, the author of Acts, says that Judas went out and bought a field and 'falling headlong, he burst open in the middle and all his bowels gushed out' (Acts 1:18). A fairly gruesome death, but one which could as easily be attributed to supernatural intervention as to Judas' own actions.

One of the other stories of suicide in the Old Testament has remarkable parallels with the story of Judas Iscariot. 2 Samuel 15–18 tells the story of the rebellion of Absalom against his father King David, and one of the key figures in the story is a man called Ahithophel. He was a key adviser to King David, but he changed sides and supported Absalom's rebellion. When it became clear that he had picked the losing side, he hanged himself (2 Samuel 17:23). Like Matthew's account of Judas' suicide, the facts of his death are told simply and starkly – the same method of death is chosen, and in both instances the text simply says that he 'hanged himself'.

In Psalm 41, which is attributed to King David, he complains that 'even my bosom friend in whom I trusted, who ate of my bread, has lifted the heel against me' (verse 9). Ancient Jewish commentary on this psalm often pointed to Ahithophel as being the bosom friend who betrayed David in his son's rebellion – but here there is a strong parallel with Jesus and Judas Iscariot. In his account of the Last Supper, Matthew reports that Jesus says he will be betrayed by one who has 'dipped his hand into the bowl' with him (Matthew 26:23) – a similar act of intimacy to eating of another's bread.

I think there are strong arguments to suggest that Matthew in his Gospel writing is deliberately drawing parallels between Jesus as the Messiah and David, the greatest anointed king of Israel. One of those parallels is the mirroring of Judas Iscariot with Ahithophel. Matthew includes the account of Judas' suicide, not to make him appear even more damned than he already was, but to draw out the links between Jesus as the Messiah and the original anointed one, King David.

When we consider what the Bible has to say about suicide, there is very little to go on – certainly not enough to create the edifice of condemnation that has been constructed against those who have taken their own lives.

2. Suicide in Christian history

The difficulty that the Church has faced over suicide is that it is a sin from which there is no opportunity to repent. This was the conclusion reached by St Augustine in one of his greatest works, *City of God*, which has formed the basis of Christian thinking in the centuries since. St Thomas Aquinas in his work *Summa Theologica* similarly describes it as a mortal sin, because there is no opportunity for repentance following it.[42] However, Protestant thinkers have tried to distance themselves from this viewpoint. John Calvin said that only one unforgiveable sin is mentioned in Scripture, which is blasphemy against the Holy Spirit (Matthew 12:31). Some have suggested that since the body is the temple of the Holy Spirit, according to 1 Corinthians 6:19, to kill yourself is to commit this blasphemy, but Calvin rejected this.

The position of the Roman Catholic Church today is similar to the view taken by most Christian denominations. According to paragraph 2283 of its Catechism:

> We should not despair of the eternal salvation of persons who have taken their own lives. By ways known to him alone, God can provide the opportunity for salutary repentance. If they are in hell, then we are reminded that God himself was in hell on Holy Saturday and reaches out to those in its very depths with the possibility of redemption. For this reason, the Church should pray for persons who have taken their own lives.

This theological standpoint is a far more helpful one to families who face the agony of a loved one having killed themselves than the Church's position in former ages. It focuses on the grace of God, not on the actions of humanity. When we consider the cross on which Jesus died, we see God's overwhelming love for all people. This is a love which can comprehend all human failure and weakness, and it does not exclude anyone from the bounds of its love. It is this which we ought to proclaim confidently to those who are confronted by the suicide of a loved one. Those who exercise ministry in funerals have rightly learnt to be very cautious about making any statements which seem to judge the eternal destiny of the one who has died. Such judgements are to be left to God, who alone can see the secrets of our

---

42. St Thomas Aquinas, *Summa Theologica*, Vol II:II 64.5.

hearts. We should certainly apply such discretion to situations of suicide as much as we do to any other death.

3. Taking a funeral service following a suicide

Under the Canons of the Church of England, ministers have a duty to conduct the funeral service of anyone who lived in their parish, was on their electoral roll, or who died in their parish. However, one of the exceptions to this rule is where a person 'of sound mind' committed suicide.[43] I am not aware of any of my colleagues today who would seek to excuse themselves from such a funeral on this ground – and it of course begs the question as to whose place it is to judge whether the person was of sound mind.

The Canon – that is the ecclesiastical law – goes on to say that where General Synod has specifically authorised a special order of service to be taken following a suicide, that special order should be used rather than the ordinary funeral service. Indeed, the Church of England website information concerning funerals states that 'The Church has special funerals for children, or after sudden or violent deaths, including suicide.'[44] However, I am not aware of particular services for these circumstances, and the websites of various dioceses do not offer any enlightenment on this subject.

I am not convinced that it would be helpful to have a different service for someone who has committed suicide. The text in the website likens the situation to the death of a child, but it is very different. At the death of a child, there is a need to acknowledge the uniqueness of the situation – a child's death is not like any other death, and this needs to be emphasised. However, even if a death by suicide is different from 'normal' deaths, it only adds pain to draw attention to this. It is hard enough to come to terms with the death of someone by suicide; to receive the message from the church that a 'normal' funeral service is not possible in these circumstances is profoundly unhelpful, and even damaging.

There are helpful prayers provided in the liturgical resources of the Roman Catholic Church, the Anglican Church and many other denominations, for use in the funeral of one who has taken his or her own life. A Roman Catholic prayer asks God 'to look gently on your servant N and by the blood of the cross forgive his/her sins and failings'.[45] This seems to have absolutely the right focus on God and his grace shown at the cross, not on the actions of the one who has died.

---

43. The Canons of the Church of England B38 (2).
44. http://www.churchofengland.org/weddings-baptisms-funerals/funerals/planning-a-funeral.aspx (accessed 23 April 2013).
45. From *Order of Christian Funerals: Rites of Committal*, London: Burns & Oates, 1990, p.131.

In Chapter 4, I spoke of the pastoral and theological benefits of using a confession as part of a funeral service. Where someone has died by suicide, this seems particularly important – to bring before God the feelings of anger and guilt that are felt towards the one who has died, and also to ask God to forgive that person. Here is a situation where von Balthasar's insights about the light of Christ being present in the furthest reaches of hell seem particularly apposite: here is a situation where we should pray that the person may know God's light and love in the hell beyond the grave, even where they could not see it in the hell of their lives on this side of death.

Solitary funerals

1. The funeral with no or few mourners

One of the first questions that I always ask a bereaved family when we meet to plan the funeral is how many people are likely to be at the service. It can be a huge comfort for a family at a funeral when they enter the church or chapel and see a church full of people wanting to support them and pay their own respects to the one who has died.

So what happens when there is no one, or very few people? Under the Public Health (Control of Diseases) Act 1984, borough councils and unitary authorities have a duty to make provision for the funerals of those who die in their area and to pay for them. The local authority will organise a public health funeral if there is nobody else to organise it. This is very much a last resort option – if anybody comes forward to arrange such a funeral, they will be responsible for covering the costs. Financial help can be available through the Social Fund, but this is only in very limited circumstances.

When a local authority organises a funeral, it should ensure that the person who has died is offered a full funeral, with a hearse to take them to the chapel and a minister of religion or other suitable official to conduct the service. There may well be times when a church minister is called upon to take such a service, even though there will be very few people there.

Equally sad is the situation where the deceased does have family, but they all live some distance away and they simply instruct the funeral director to arrange a committal for their loved one at the crematorium without any ceremony or formal funeral. It is unlikely that we as church ministers will get involved in such services because the undertaker is never instructed to notify a local minister. Good funeral directors will give such a person the respect and honour that they give to everyone whose funeral they carry out and will always insist on being present in the crematorium chapel as the words of committal are read, and perhaps would say the Lord's Prayer or another suitable prayer as part of the committal process. In death, nobody is 'just a shell' – they are a person who deserves respect and honour in death, and we should be grateful to funeral directors who recognise this for those who die alone.

On those occasions when we are called to assist at a public health funeral where there are no mourners present, how does it differ from an ordinary funeral? In some ways it should not differ too much – the person who has died is as much the loved creation and child of God as one who dies surrounded by family and friends who will all come to fill the chapel in support. However, the difference has been made particularly stark due to the changes in funeral practice over the last 20 years. Now that funerals focus on giving thanks for the life of the person who has died, and there are ordinarily tributes from family and friends where we find out all about the person's life, it is very hard to conduct a funeral where we know nothing of that. A life has been lived, full of incidents, full of relationships, and we know nothing of it. There may well have been a triggering event that caused them to end up on their own; there may be family with whom they lost touch through the years. It is likely that we will know none of that.

In these circumstances, some of the words of the Psalms remind us that even those who are unknown to anyone else are known to God. The opening words of Psalm 90 seem appropriate here:

> Lord, you have been our dwelling-place in all generations.
> Before the mountains were brought forth,
> or ever you had formed the earth and the world,
> from everlasting to everlasting you are God.
> You turn us back to dust,
> and say, 'Turn back you mortals'.
> For a thousand years in your sight
> are like yesterday when it is past,
> or like a watch in the night.

Or these verses from Psalm 139

> O Lord, you have searched me and known me.
> You know when I sit down and when I rise up;
> you discern my thoughts from far away . . .
> For it was you who formed my inward parts;
> you knit me together in my mother's womb.
> I praise you, for I am fearfully and wonderfully made.
> Wonderful are your works; that I know very well.
> My frame was not hidden from you,
> when I was being made in secret,
> intricately woven in the depths of the earth.
> Your eyes beheld my unformed substance.
> In your book were written
> all the days that were formed for me.

Even when we know nothing about the person who has died, we can proclaim our faith in the God who knows our goings out and our comings in, and who has known us throughout all generations. In commending a person who has died alone, we remind ourselves that they have not been abandoned by God.

2. The despised or hated person

One of the first things the widow said to me as I walked through the door was, 'Well, I don't know what you are going to say about him. He was a horrible man and I hated him.' On that particular occasion, there were at least family and some friends who turned out to pay their respects, but it was clear that this was not a man who had been held in any great affection by those around him. Nonetheless, the widow looked to me to give him a eulogy and offer some hope.

At funerals, we expect a eulogy to be given and for all the good points in the person's life to be highlighted. For an unpopular person, although it may not be a funeral where nobody is gathered, it is likely that the gathering will be very small. What do we do when we are all too aware of the failings of that person – perhaps because they were a convicted criminal, on the sex offenders' register, or someone who was seen as a bad neighbour and a public nuisance?

The most important thing that we should do as ministers on these occasions is to remind ourselves of Jesus' words of rebuke to the scribes and Pharisees when he ate with tax collectors and 'sinners'. He said to them in Mark 2:17, 'I have come to call not the righteous but sinners.'

There is a danger that we see the purpose of a funeral as the retelling of a person's story as the greatest gift to the local community that has ever lived. At the heart of the Christian faith is the reminder that we are saved not by our own righteousness but by God's saving grace. We know God's grace extends to all – even to the dying thief on the cross – so there is no need to fear taking the funeral of someone of whom we are more aware of their failings than their strengths.

Indeed, there can be something very liberating about it. Sometimes I come away from a funeral at which a number of eulogies have been extolling endlessly the virtues of the deceased, and I fear that they have ceased to be human. One thing that I am absolutely certain of in myself is my failures and my weaknesses – it is part of being human – and when no acknowledgement is given of that in a person's eulogy, they become something of a plaster saint rather than a flesh-and-blood human being.

One of the wonderful things about the Christian faith which we should not fear to proclaim boldly is that God meets us in our weakness, not in our strength. If we are asked to carry out a funeral for an unpopular person, we can have the courage to be honest about the very mixed emotions and memories that will be experienced by those who have come. A prayer of confession, together with a time of quiet for those who are there, will allow the mourners to deal honestly with the various emotions that they feel at such a time. We do not need to give lurid details of the horrors of the person's life – silence or quiet music will allow people to think through their own painful memories and commit them to God.

Big public funerals

There is little that needs to be said about the opposite problem, but such funerals can be just as difficult to conduct. It may well be that at a funeral where there are several hundred people, the family will want a number of people to give a tribute. If four tributes are given, those paying them may well feel that unless they speak for at least ten minutes, they will not have done justice to their much-loved friend or relative. Immediately it can be seen that the congregation is being asked to sit through at least 40 minutes of eulogies, which is more than most people can do. As I said above, I think it also runs the very severe danger of making the person we honour less human, not more so, because they are painted in increasingly glowing terms.

All that can be said in these circumstances is how important it is to be realistic with the family when planning the funeral. Some ministers insist on seeing the text of anything that is to be read at a funeral they are conducting so that they can see if it is going to last too long. This may not be feasible, but it is important to stress with the family that if there are to be multiple tributes, none of them should last for more than five minutes. There will be times when we get that wrong, and in those circumstances, all we can do is hope and pray that the service provided comfort for the family. Some of the funerals that I have conducted for much-loved members of my own congregation have been badly out of shape because of the tributes that were paid – and yet they were still able to be an enormous source of comfort for the family. As I said in Chapter 4, our role is not to provide beautiful liturgy; it is to offer support and help to a family in need.

Undoubtedly, the most difficult aspect of dealing with a very big, public funeral is where there is media interest in the person's death – perhaps because the person was well-known locally or nationally, or because the death caught the national headlines. Most church denominations will be able to offer support at a regional or national level in these circumstances. If the local or national press contact you about a person's funeral – or you are aware that press cameras will be present – it is always worth contacting the church press office to ask for their advice. In these circumstances, you should certainly work with them, not on your own.

There will be all sorts of funerals that are difficult. In many ways, we only know what they are once we have experienced them. They will be the funerals that you remember afterwards – and they are often the funerals from which we gain the most. Difficult funerals remind us what a privilege it is to conduct this ministry, because families are very aware of the difficulty of the situation and need the help of someone who can help guide them through. That is our role at all funerals, and it is extremely humbling to hear that we have made a difference to people at an awful time in their lives. Never is this more true in our society today than following the death of a child, and it is to this that we turn now.

Eight
The death of children

By Dorothy Moore Brooks
Chaplain, Great Ormond Street Hospital for Sick Children

Introduction: something is wrong!

My grandfather, who was born in the east end of Glasgow in 1900, was one of six children. However, only three of them survived to reach their tenth birthday. This particular family story would not have been newsworthy in its day. Rather it would have been a story similar to that of many other friends and neighbours, and is a reasonably accurate reflection of the childhood mortality rates at that time. In the Victorian era as a whole, half of all live births were followed by death within the first year.

A century later, such tragic stories and stark statistics send a shockwave through us. Today, if three children out of a family of six were to die, society would rightly regard it as a rare and enormous personal tragedy and it would be front-page news. We simply do not expect our children to die before us. It goes against the natural order. Everything within us cries out that it is wrong. I remember one mother, whose child was dying and whom I met in the children's hospital where I work, articulating this so clearly. She said this: 'I planned for many things in her life – her first day at school, her wedding – but never, in my worst nightmare, did I plan for her funeral.'

I have often thought about my great-grandparents and wondered how they coped with the searing pain which such a litany of loss must have inflicted upon them. That little is known about this situation in our family, other than the bare facts of it, perhaps gives us a clue as to how people coped – silently and in isolation. Was it made any easier by the harsh reality that it was not uncommon to bury your children? Does the expectation that you may lose a child lessen the pain of that loss when it becomes a reality? I cannot imagine that the answer to any of these questions is 'yes'. Instead, I can only assume that their lives, and the lives of so many others like them, were irrevocably changed by the deaths of their beloved children. Perhaps, in an era when talking therapies, support groups and specialist bereavement services and charities such as those we have recourse to today, were unheard of, bereaved parents simply had to find a way to integrate the sorrowful music of their losses as an accompaniment to their lives from then on.

The death of a child is wrong and defies the natural order that we can reasonably expect to experience in our lives. Children bury their parents, and when this order is reversed, a deep-seated confusion sets in and affects the journey through grief. As those trying to accompany and provide pastoral support for people whose lives have been devastated by such a loss, we must understand this. Bereaved parents will need to tell and retell the story in order to begin to try to make sense of a loss of which little sense can be made. A key part of our role is to be present with them, to listen to them and to walk with them as they journey through the complex and arduous path of grieving for their child.

Perhaps it is inevitable that many parents who have lost a child will ask why this has happened to them and why their child has died. Even if they are not asking, 'Why us?' they may be asking other why questions: why, in a modern era when medical science is so advanced, should a child die? Why would a loving God allow such sorrow?

None of us can know the answer to the existential question of why their child has died. Beyond the physical reasons for the death of their child, we have to accept a difficult truth that does not sit easily with those of us in pastoral ministry who like to fix things. This uncomfortable and unsettling truth is that there can be no reasonable explanation or acceptable answer to the bigger 'Why?' question which will resonate honestly with a bereaved person, because the death of a child defies any explanation. We who try to offer one run the risk of being insensitive fools!

If we are to understand the death of a child within a theological framework and offer appropriate and sensitive pastoral care to bereaved parents, these words of God through the prophet Isaiah are a good place to start.

> No more shall there be in it an infant that lives but a few days, or an old person who does not live out a lifetime . . . They shall not labour in vain, or bear children for calamity; for they will be offspring blessed by the Lord – and their descendants as well. *Isaiah 65:20, 23*

In my role as a paediatric hospital chaplain, which inevitably involves supporting bereaved, or soon-to-be bereaved, parents, Isaiah's vision of the new heaven and the new earth gives me pastoral confidence to say that the death of a child simply cannot be within God's created order. Like us, the heavens cry out that this is wrong. God weeps with the mother or father who has lost their child, and he grieves with the sibling whose brother or sister has died.

We must, of course, acknowledge the value of those whom Isaiah calls the 'infant that lives but a few days' and the 'children [borne] for calamity'. That their lives are short does not mean that they are therefore worth less than one who has their full span of years. Many of these children have a profound effect on those around them and they bring joy and blessing, no matter how short their life is. Viktor Frankl, the twentieth-century Austrian psychiatrist, neurologist and writer, puts this beautifully and with a soothing pastoral sensitivity when he asserts that:

> We cannot, after all, judge a biography by its length, by the number of pages in it; we must judge by the richness of the contents . . . Sometimes the 'unfinisheds' are among the most beautiful symphonies.[46]

However, no matter how much is achieved or how many lives are touched by the short life of a child, we must also accept that their premature death is not within God's good plan for his people. When the kingdom of God breaks in, one of the 'never agains' and 'no mores' of which we read in Revelation must surely be the death of a child. 'He will wipe every tear from their eyes. Death will be no more; mourning and crying and pain will be no more, for the first things have passed away' (Revelation 21:4).

In the face of the death of a child, we may be tempted to hide behind Jesus' words in Mark 10 and Matthew 19 where he puts the disciples straight about their tendency to block children's access to him: 'Let the little children come to me, and do not stop them; for it is to such as these that the kingdom of heaven belongs' (Matthew 19:14 and Mark 10:14). Let us be clear. Jesus is not talking about the death of children here, but is instead doing two things First, he is teaching his listeners that the gospel is for all people, children included. Age is no barrier to experiencing God and reflecting his kingdom. Secondly, he wants the disciples to understand that the simple, transparent and trusting faith of a child is something that they should aspire to and learn from.

There are times when I use this passage as a child is dying to remind parents that the God who weeps with them in their searing pain is also a God whose gentle arms are wide open, ready to welcome their child. It would, however, be pastorally crass and theologically inaccurate to use these words of Jesus to suggest to those parents that it is God's will for their child to die.

One Friday morning I was asked to go to the intensive care unit to baptise a 4-year-old boy who had been admitted overnight. He had contracted viral meningitis and the medical team were now sure that there was no hope of recovery. As I entered the unit, I could see a small gathering of family outside the boy's cubicle. Jamie's grandmother turned and, as she saw me approach, she shouted, 'How can you come in here and talk to us of a God of love, when he is lying dying in there?'

---

46. Viktor E. Frankl, *The Doctor and the Soul: From Psychotherapy to Logotherapy*, London: Souvenir Press Ltd, 2004, p.66.

Her son, Jamie's dad, said, 'Mum, you can't talk to the vicar like that!' to which I replied that she could and maybe she needed to tell me how angry she was.

At that point, the woman fell into my arms and sobbed. Through the flood of tears she told me of her delightful little grandson who had been fine until a few days ago, running round the park, full of life and boundless energy. She told me of her deep sorrow, not only at seeing her grandson so ill, but also of the agony of watching her son and his wife so broken by this sudden tragedy which had engulfed them. She asked what kind of God would do this to them. That was not a question I could answer, but in time we began to talk about a God who also knew the agony of losing a much-loved son one Friday, and whose love for them and for Jamie might be glimpsed in his presence and his tears.

After a while, we went in to see Jamie. I baptised him and then committed him into God's hands for safe keeping. It was awful but, for a few minutes at least, there was a peace in that room and a tangible awareness of God holding this family in their broken-heartedness.

At such times of immeasurable suffering such as this, or when we are invited to conduct the funeral of a child, we need to be clear about what we believe and be confident in expressing it. 'Let the little children come to me' were important words to say during that baptism, and many others like it, not to assert that God had plucked Jamie out from the crowd because he wanted another little angel in heaven. Rather, these words were helpful because they could go some way to assuring this distraught family that the God who was with them today had his arms wide open ready to receive Jamie when the brokenness of this world meant that they had no choice but to let him go.

What is different about a child's funeral?

So what, if anything, is, can or should be different about the funeral of a child from that of an adult?

Perhaps, to follow on from our theological framework, the first thing is to be honest about how wrong this feels and is. We believe it, everyone is feeling it, so surely it is right to articulate those thoughts and feelings. We are not praying to a God who has sent this disaster; we pray to a God who weeps with us in this tragedy and who promises to be with us in it.

1. Siblings

One of the ways in which a child's funeral will be different from an adult's is that, in many cases, there will be siblings who are themselves still children. If this is the case, then we need to remember that they are grieving too and may want to contribute something to the planning of their brother or sister's funeral, and be involved in some way in the day itself. In order for this to be possible, and helpful rather than harmful, they need to be prepared for what will happen. They may want to enact the funeral through play, e.g. by making a lego coffin or requisitioning a toy truck to be used as a hearse. This will inevitably be difficult for the adults in the family to cope with, visualising what will happen and enabling understanding through age-appropriate explanations, but it is vital to the children being confident that they can cope with the day. Simple, clear answers to their questions about what will happen in the service and to the body is a way to help alleviate the child's fears.

It is important that we ask if and how brothers and sisters can be included in what will be a very hard and potentially bewildering day for them. They may not want to do anything in the service, but they can be part of the planning – perhaps in terms of choices of music, photographs for the order of service or, more commonly now, a projected slideshow, or other details that will make the funeral personal and helpful.

On an emotional level, children need to know that people might be sad, and this will enable them to understand that they can be sad too. Parents sometimes express a worry that if their children come to the funeral, they will not feel able to grieve honestly, but the reality is that a family needs to find a way to deal honestly with their grief, and a part of that is grieving together.

At 12-month-old Isabel's funeral (whose story we will hear more of later in this chapter), her 3-year-old sister Phoebe had a special part to play. Mum Pippa explained how they involved her:

> We explained to Phoebe that we were going to have a special service at church to say goodbye to Isabel and to say thank you to God for giving her to us even though it wasn't for as long as we would have hoped. I explained that I was going to stand at the front and say something about Isabel. I asked Phoebe if she would like to say something too and she said she would, so we wrote a few short sentences about Isabel, and Phoebe practised saying them until she knew them. I thought she would be too shy and wouldn't say it when it came to it, but she did. I held her and she said them in front of everyone – my little girl who normally won't even go up with Sunday school to show the congregation what they did that week. I was very proud of her and I think it helped her to feel involved. I also think when she looks back she will be proud of herself. She also chose a hymn for the service . . . I wanted her to feel as comfortable with it as she could and to express herself.

12-year-old Emily's family (who also tell more of their story later) chose to have the prayer of committal outside the church before the hearse drove the coffin away to the crematorium.

> We asked Emily's friends to write a message to her and these were tied to the strings of 20 red balloons outside the church at the end of the service. Emily's 1-year-old sister, Olivia, released the first balloon. Emily's Mum Bridget said, 'We wanted her to play a part in the service should she ever ask "Where was I?" when she gets older.'

Olivia is unlikely to have her own memories of this act. It may be hard for her in years to come to be unable to remember her sister, but her significant part in saying goodbye to Emily will be part of the family narrative of the day which will assure her that she was there, that she was included and that she mattered.

There are many other ways in which siblings can be actively and positively involved in the funeral of their brother or sister. 12-year-old Jason wrote an acrostic of his sister Julie's name to explain all the things he would miss about her, and this was read out in her funeral service. He said afterwards that he felt proud that his words were included. His family all had a say in the choice of coffin and were all happy with their joint decision that Julie should be buried in a painted rainbow coffin.

5-year-old Sophie's little brother Sam died at just a few days old and she felt very sad because she and Sam would never be able to play together. The family chose a cardboard coffin and, in the days before the funeral, Sophie and her parents spent time together drawing pictures on it. As well as making the coffin look pretty, it also gave them time to talk about Sam in a non-threatening way. When the funeral came, Sophie was less afraid to be near the coffin and was happy that she had done something so special for her little brother Sam.

All of these things, and countless other creative ideas which families may want to do, may seem like small, insignificant or even upsetting acts to others. However, they can be of huge significance to bereaved siblings as they struggle to manage their feelings of loss and attend what for many will be their first funeral. Making room for them to be involved is vital and can help them deal with their often complex feelings and find a language with which to say goodbye to their brother or sister.

2. Grandparents

Another relevant but often forgotten way in which a child's funeral is different from that of an adult is that there may be grandparents. It is important to make special mention of them because the grandparents of a deceased child have a unique and complex path to walk. In one respect, they have a double whammy. Not only are they grieving for a much-loved grandchild, but they also know the agony of watching their own child suffer intense pain at the loss of their child. The feelings of helplessness, which are an inevitable part of witnessing this sorrow, coupled with their own grief, are a heavy burden to bear.

A grandparent may find it hard to acknowledge their own emotional, practical or spiritual needs, assuming that they are much less valid or important than those of the child's parents. Their priority may rightly be in supporting their son or daughter and the rest of the family through this nightmare. Too often the cost of this, though, is that their own grief is hidden away, unacknowledged or put on hold, and the results of this can do untold damage. Those of us seeking to support the family bereaved of a child must be aware of the grief of grandparents, take time to seek them out, encourage them to find time, space and appropriate support to acknowledge and express their own grief.

3. Content and choices

The content of a child's funeral will rightly be different from that of an adult. Perhaps the fact that the person for whom we gather to give thanks and grieve is a child gives us permission to throw the rule book away and dispense with many of the traditional expectations that we have for a funeral. If our world has been turned upside down by this tragedy which flies in the face of the natural order, then surely the least we should have are some creative and child-centred choices.

Sadly, some clergy are so fazed at the thought of a child's funeral that the only acknowledgement they make that it is a child is to say the set prayers for the funeral of a child from whatever funeral order they are using. Of course, the need to give thanks, the need to grieve and the need to find meaning, comfort and hope are vital for a funeral to be helpful, no matter whose funeral it is. However, what I have learned from doing many children's funerals is that there are good pastoral and theological reasons to make it different. We run the risk of doing great harm to the family if the funeral of their beloved child is little different from that of their elderly great aunt. Paradoxically, I have also learned that some of the things that are done at a child's funeral can also be helpful at an adult's funeral.

If a family wants floral tributes, it will soon become clear that large floral arrangements will swamp a small coffin. An alternative is to encourage family and friends to each bring a single flower and, as part of the service, to bring their flowers forward and place them on or around the coffin. This also gives another opportunity to come near to and/or touch the coffin and provides an opportunity for each person to say their own goodbye.

When a wicker coffin is used, or a standard coffin with handles, it is possible to tie coloured ribbons onto the wicker or handles. Cardboard coffins can be decorated or have messages written on them. These are just a few examples of ways in which people can be encouraged to gather close to the child, to express their love, gratitude and sorrow for that child, to do something tangible as an aid to prayer and to have the opportunity to say their own goodbye. If we lead the way with this by not being afraid to touch the coffin ourselves, then others may feel more at ease to do so too.

Many parents want to carry their child into the church, chapel or to the graveside. This practice is neither new nor exclusive to the funeral of a child. However, the reason for doing so at a child's funeral may be very different. Parents may want to carry their child, no matter what their age, on this last journey because part of what we do for our children in the vulnerable moments of their lives – when they are sick, upset or asleep – is to carry them. Why would we not want to carry them in death too?

When our first child Matthew was stillborn, my husband wanted to carry our tiny son into the church. I had carried him in the womb during my pregnancy, but he had never had the opportunity to carry his child. For him, being able to carry his son into church was a symbolic way of bringing him to God, and this would be the only opportunity for this to happen. Though we had not anticipated this at the time of planning the service, doing this also reminded us that God, as our loving parent, was carrying us through such a traumatic and vulnerable time.

Parents' voices

Parents will often have special reasons for the choices they make for their child's funeral, and we need to give them time and space to express what matters to them. Over the years I have had the privilege of sharing the journey with many families who have known the sorrowful and lonely walk of losing a child. What often astounds, moves and humbles me is that, from the chaos the heart-wrenching grief, bewilderment and trauma that the death of their beloved child has brought into their lives, emerges an extraordinary, instinctive clarity and creative energy in the form of how they want their child's funeral to be.

Stories help us to see the principles of good practice at work, therefore it is surely right that the voices of two sets of bereaved parents take centre stage here. Two families will now speak for themselves as they describe how they negotiated their way through the many decisions that had to be made for the funerals of their children. Their voices are the ones that have the greatest credibility, and they are the best teachers when it comes to helping us to learn what pastoral help and support families need at such a painful time.

Isabel's funeral

12-month-old Isabel's Mum, Pippa, explains what was important to her family as they planned the funeral of their daughter.

> Isabel had been highly medicalised during her life as she had been born with a number of problems. I wanted her to be as natural as possible in death. Within hours of her death, the words, 'I want her to be a tree,' had come out of my mouth. A close friend had had an aunt buried in a woodland burial ground and suggested it to us. We investigated and went to see two. The one we chose is an old wood and it felt right as soon as we arrived. My husband Mark spent much of his youth cycling in the woods, and when he feels sad or stressed, going for a walk in the woods always calms him, so I felt it was especially right for both of us. It also meant we can take Phoebe and go for a walk in the woods where we feel close to Isabel without standing and staring at a grave. We have had a wooden plaque with a carved robin placed to mark where she is, and Phoebe loves to stroke the robin and help Daddy to oil it. It gives them both something physical to do when we visit, which helps them a lot. One of the hardest things we found is that when you lose a child, there is nothing 'to do'.
>
> It was important to me that I had as much as possible to do with the process of burying Isabel. I felt that as her mother it was my job to care for her, and that didn't end at the point she died. I prepared her body, dressed her and placed her in her coffin. I know this wouldn't be for everyone, especially as she had had a post-mortem, but for me it was something I needed to do. Isabel's Godmother, who was a nurse, helped me. It had been me who had dealt with the majority of Isabel's medical care and for me this was a continuation of caring for her body. It took me ages to decide what she should wear. I was very worried that she would be cold, and although I knew it was illogical, I couldn't help but wrap her up warm. Mark, who is a doting father cared for her spirit, and for him, once she had died, her body was no longer her and he found it hard to see her body, so he left this to me. It was important for each of us to do what we needed to and to acknowledge that this was different for each of us.
>
> We had a short service in a room at the woods and then we carried her coffin to her grave. Mark and I wanted to carry the coffin but it was quite heavy, so Mark's brother and a close friend helped us. They were the most physically able to do this and I felt I could rely on them to manage their grief and be emotionally able to do this. Our friends and family came with us to the grave where Mark and I lowered her into it, we said

a prayer and everyone threw in a rose. They then all left and Mark and I filled in the grave on our own. Again, this gave Mark something physical to do for his baby girl that he felt good at. My best friend said to me as she left, 'You tuck her in nice and tight,' and I said, 'I always do.' It did represent putting her to bed one last time. I wanted to leave her in the woods as she was going to be, rather than a stranger coming and doing things after we left. As we walked away the sun shone on her grave and the flowers we had left looked beautiful. It felt like a safe place for her to be.

Like Mark and Pippa, many bereaved parents express or feel some concern that their child will somehow be alone in death, so encouraging them to be close to or touch the coffin may be important and bring some comfort to them. Prior to the funeral, the family may want to place special toys, teddy bears, cards or family photos into the coffin. As the officiating minister, I kneel beside the child's coffin and lay my hand on it as I say the words of commendation or committal.

Emily's funeral

Emily's Mum, Bridget, explained some of the choices their family made when they were planning Emily's funeral. In her words, they wanted to make sure every part of the service 'could be traced back to Emily'.

> My mind had drifted into thoughts about her funeral, and although I never discussed death with her, I made notes for myself about the things that were important to her. The things that rocked Emily's world were her friends, her music, her rabbit 'Peppa Boo-Boo Kibble' (real name!) and sweets.
>
> We also knew Emily had a passion for green issues. Emily embraced the philosophy of Re-use, Reduce & Recycle taught by her beloved year 4 teacher. We knew our local green burial ground was where Emily should go. However, on a tour of their 'service hall', it was very clear their offer was not right for us. It was too small, cold, empty and felt removed from God.
>
> We wanted a church service with a gentle Christian message of hope, with a green funeral director and a private cremation. We had support from Emily's school who invited all the pupils in her year to attend provided they were accompanied by a parent. Staff members, including the headmaster, also attended.
>
> What helped was the support of our vicar who took time to understand Emily when we prepared her eulogy, was involved in all the decision making and discussions with the school and with the funeral home. He understood that all of the choices we made had an important meaning, even if we were not able to articulate them at the time.
>
> We chose to have Emily cremated privately after the service at the church, mainly due to the logistics of the day. We had the option of

having the cremation before the service but we felt we wanted Emily at the church in her 'earthly form'. This led to some amusement when her coffin was placed at the altar. We chose a cardboard coffin inside a one-size-fits-all oak casket. This was explained to the children: Emily was in a cardboard coffin because it was kinder to the environment and that Emily had not grown taller since she passed.

We chose hymns associated with Emily's schools and one chosen by Jessica (Emily's older sister) who had fond memories of singing it at school.

The funeral choices made by families, such as those whose voices we have heard in this chapter, are made to recognise, honour and celebrate the unique life, value and impact that their child's life had, and to recognise the huge gap that their premature death leaves. Emily's mum Bridget sums this up beautifully: 'We had a daughter, Emily. She was here and she was loved.'

Conclusion

What is so different about a child's funeral? The key difference is that their existence speaks of a broken creation in which events happen which are far removed from the good world which God made. The comfort we can offer at such funerals is that we are in the presence of a God who identifies with the pain of this loss; he knows the sorrow of watching his Son die. The truth we can offer is that, in the way he encountered children, Jesus made it clear that they are close to the heart of God and are welcomed by him. We need not be afraid of doing childlike things in the service and including child-focused content. Indeed, we must do so! The hope we can offer is that when our prayers are finally answered and God's kingdom comes in all its fullness, Isaiah's words will be our reality and 'no more shall there be . . . an infant that lives but a few days,' nor will we 'bear children for calamity.'

I am hugely grateful to the families of both Isabel and Emily who have allowed me to accompany them a little as they grieve for their lovely girls, and who have generously shared their stories with me for this chapter.

With the exception of Isabel and Emily's families, all other names have been changed.

Nine

When the day is over – pastoral care for the bereaved

Since the change in regulations in 2003 facilitating the use of civil celebrants to conduct funerals, there has been an increase of interest in the planning of services. The internet offers a bewildering array of comments and resources – as well as insights from faith groups, there are professional organisations of civil celebrants, humanists, funeral directors and many other interested groups of people.

There are also vast numbers of blogs on the web where those who have an interest in funerals leave comments and have conversations about various aspects of funeral services. It may seem extraordinary to think that people would want to spend their time discussing funerals, but anyone who has spent time with a group of clergy and asked them to talk about funerals will know that it is not so unusual – they become very animated by the subject!

One of my favourite blogs from the UK is entitled 'The Good Funeral Guide'.[47] It is run by Charles Cowling as a not-for-profit social enterprise. His concern is to improve the quality of funerals in this country and to provide a blog on which people can comment on good practice. Looking through the blog, it is clear that many regular contributors are civil celebrants who are keen to exchange ideas and offer good practice, as well as funeral directors and interested lay people.

These blogs cover all sorts of aspects of a funeral and list categories of conversations on the blog from the bureaucracy surrounding funerals to novel ideas for green funerals and alternative methods of body disposal. However, there is one aspect of funerals which is not discussed, and seems to me to be a glaring omission from most funeral discussions: pastoral care after the funeral.

When a person dies, the family does not just 'move on' after the service. Often they do not need the support and help of professionals in the same way, but they are still left coping with the death of a loved one. Often it is much more difficult once the funeral is over: up to that point they receive the support of friends, and there is a lot to do concerning the planning of the funeral and the other arrangements surrounding the death. But once the funeral is finished, there can be an awful sense of loneliness.

---

47. http://www.goodfuneralguide.co.uk/blog/ (accessed 24 April 2013).

I think this is one aspect of bereavement and funerals where a church must continue to offer support. One of the saddest aspects of the fact that the Church is no longer conducting the numbers of funerals it did previously is that the ongoing pastoral support that should be a part of every church's ministry has also disappeared. Civil celebrants can offer an excellent funeral service, and professional bodies such as the Institute of Civil Funerals and other professional bodies for civil celebrants offer good training on how to conduct a good funeral. But that is the extent of their interest in the funeral – civil celebrants do not offer ongoing pastoral care to those who are bereaved.

In this chapter, I want to look at ways in which a church can do this as part of its funeral ministry. However, there are two things that should be stressed at the outset.

1. Although churches should be in a position to offer ongoing pastoral support, I think frequently they fail in this task. Beyond a cursory phone call from the minister a couple of weeks after the funeral, many bereaved families do not feel that anything was offered by the church. In many cases, the bereaved receive the support they need from their family networks and close friends. If we are to take funeral ministry seriously in the Church, I think we need to look at ways in which we can do more.
2. In recognising that we should do more for families, as responsible ministers we must also recognise those occasions when more specialist help is needed. Sometimes our role should be to put the bereaved in touch with bereavement counsellors, such as the service offered by Cruse, or organisations supporting bereaved parents. In many areas there are local networks of support, and it is important that ministers know what these are.

Aware, then, that we should do more, but also knowing that very often the more that we can offer is not enough, in what ways can we as church ministers offer pastoral support to families?

Pastoral support around the time of death

The death of a loved one can cause many different physical and spiritual, as well as emotional, reactions. A bereaved person may be unable to sleep, they may become anxious or depressed, they may feel a tightness around their chest, they may feel a burning sense of anger against God or the universe that this tragedy has overtaken them. If someone who had recently been bereaved complained of any of these symptoms, most of us would point to their recent bereavement as one of the causes of these feelings.

There are myriad books about the stages of grief and, as ministers to those who are bereaved, it is important that we are aware of these. It is not the purpose of this book to provide expertise on counselling and bereavement theory – there are many other resources that can be used for that. However, it is appropriate in any book on funerals to speak about the pastoral care that we should provide to the bereaved, in the light of the knowledge that we have.

Put simply, pastoral care for the bereaved is about being attentive to their whole self and providing support for them. The Church may feel that it has a particular role to play in considering the spiritual needs of the bereaved because that aspect of humanity has become marginalised and is seen as the domain of specialists, of whom we are one. Nonetheless, any good pastor would also be attentive to the physical and emotional symptoms displayed by the bereaved and want to ensure that those needs are being met appropriately.

But what of the care that we offer for people's spiritual needs? The story told in the previous chapter by Dorothy Moore Brooks offers a telling example of people's needs – of a grandmother hurling her accusation at a hospital chaplain, whom she fears will 'come here and talk to us of a God of love, when he is lying dying in there?' This grandmother articulates in acute form the spiritual crisis that we face at death, but that most people will not vocalise. The pastoral care that we offer in supporting people's spiritual needs is about allowing them to speak those questions in anger, and allowing their voices to be heard.

The crisis caused by death brings about this kind of spiritual need. It will not always be as acutely felt or stated as in the example above – when a person dies old and full of years, released from a period of suffering or poor quality of life, the spiritual questions we face are not so acute as they are with the death of a child. But we still face spiritual questions, because issues about the meaning of life and death surface in us all. The key element of pastoral care in attending to people's spiritual needs at death is in helping them make sense of the meaning of this particular death.

In 1993, a book entitled *Intoxicated by my Illness*, was posthumously published, having been written by the American essayist and reviewer, Anatole Broyard. It is a slim book of only some 135 pages and deals with Broyard's reflections and feelings on being diagnosed with terminal prostate cancer. As he writes about the meaning of death, he comments, 'Once we had a narrative of heaven and hell, but now we make our own narratives.'[48]

---

48. Anatole Broyard, *Intoxicated by my Illness and other writings on life and death*, New York: Ballantyne Books, 1993, p.42.

I think this sentence encapsulates the spiritual crisis that people face when confronted with death. What is the meaning of death in a society that no longer holds on to an over-arching story of the meaning of life? As Broyard comments, society tells us we have to make our own stories now.

The role of the Christian pastor is to show people the story of God and its place in the stories of people's lives. This can only be done by listening attentively to people's own stories: it is not achieved by shutting those stories down and insisting that they hear only the story we want to tell. However, neither does it mean being so sensitive to their story that we endorse everything about their own narrative. In the story from Chapter 8, while Dorothy had to hear the grandmother's anger and pain, it was also right that she talked with the family of a God whose own son died, and whose son lived in the midst of human pain and shared people's tears as well as their joys.

The hardest aspect for most clergy in offering good pastoral care to people in their need is the remembrance that this care comes through from relationship with the people, not just the delivery of spoken truths. We are trained to preach truths from the pulpit, and it is easy to see our role as delivering the truths of God's story in verbal form. But as one commentator points out, God came as the Word made flesh – not simply to deliver words, but to live as flesh and so 'the communication of Christian truth is relational and not propositional'.[49] In other words, we point people to God not simply by the words we say, but by the way in which we live our lives in relation to them.

It is here that we help people make sense of the journey through grief. We are not simply there to help people get through a ritual: if we were, then we would not offer anything more than many civil celebrants, who do a very good job in planning the ceremony and leaving the bereaved feeling that their loved one has had a good send-off. Our role as Christian ministers is to help people face the spiritual questions that arise and offer relationship with them that will help them find answers.

This begins in the turmoil of death and bereavement when our role is to help people navigate their way through the questions, while assisting in the performance of the ritual of the funeral. However, the mistake is to think that our role comes to an end after that. It is here that the Church has a distinct part to play in helping people find their way to their spiritual questions and their place within the greater story of God's interaction with the world.

The Church as a whole can play a distinctive role because it can invite into community people who are left lonely by the death of a

---

49. David Lyall, *Integrity of Pastoral Care*, London: SPCK, 2001, p.96.

loved one. It is within a community that sense can begin to be made of the questions that surround death. In the churches where I have ministered as the parish priest, more people have come into the life of the church through funerals than through any other aspect of the church's life. This is not the reason why we offer good pastoral care, but if what we are doing is showing people something more of God's love for them, it is unsurprising if they are drawn into his family and want to find out more.

It is vital, then, that, where funerals are not taken by clergy who are part of an obvious church community, ways are found for the local community to support the bereaved family. There are often situations when a funeral is booked but local ministers are unable to take the service, so a more specialist minister is brought in. Often these ministers are retired from parish life, or they may be part of a chaplaincy team that operates in a given area. They ensure that every family has the opportunity for a funeral to be taken by a church minister if they would like, rather than being told that the local minister is not available and so relying on the ministry of a civil celebrant by default. Where clergy are acting as funeral chaplains in this way, it is so important to ensure that the family of the one who has died is referred back to their local church community. It may decide that it needs no further contact, or does not want it, but that opportunity should be made available for them.

Pastoral care after the funeral

One of the stories that Dorothy tells in Chapter 8 is our own, following the stillbirth of our first son, Matthew, in 2000. We were referred by the hospital where he was born to an organisation called SANDS (Stillbirth and Neonatal Death Society). There were various local branches of SANDS that met monthly, and Dorothy and I attended for a while after Matthew died. At each meeting there was a group of up to a dozen people – some of whom had come as couples; some on their own. At each meeting, each person took a turn to talk about their own experience of having a child die. Each person's situation was different – some knew that their child had a fatal illness before birth, some had chosen to bring the pregnancy to an end as a result of that, others had no idea that anything was wrong until the pregnancy had come to term. Although our stories were all slightly different, we all listened to one another and found ways in which all the stories resonated with each other.

I attended those meetings for four or five months before deciding that I did not want to go any more. Others only came once, while for some people it was a lifeline that lasted much longer. Nobody in the room was an expert: we all simply shared a common aspect to our life's journeys. It was enough to be with others who had gone through something similar and to feel that we had permission to speak about how we were feeling. The common fears and experiences that all bereaved people share – that their friends do not want to hear them going on still about how they are feeling, that others will cross the road to avoid a conversation – were ours as bereaved parents, too. It was a great source of relief to know that people were there who would listen.

The following year, Dorothy and I moved to my first parish as vicar of Hoddesdon in east Hertfordshire. There we discovered that there was already in place a Bereavement Support Group, which operated in a similar way. After the clergy had taken a funeral, they – or one of the facilitators of the group – would make contact with the family to ask if they would like the opportunity to join the group. On many occasions, the bereaved did not accept the support then – they had their family around them, and that was enough. But every year a number of new people would attend the monthly meetings. Some would stay for a few meetings; others remained part of the group for more than a year.

Like the SANDS group, at each meeting people had the opportunity to tell their own story and be supported by the others there, in the knowledge that they, too, had experienced similar things and were not going to 'cross the road to avoid conversation'. At the end of the meeting, the facilitator gave a brief reading or meditation and prayer, as a way of acknowledging the spiritual questions that existed for those in the group.

This seems to me to be a very good example of a way in which ongoing pastoral support can be offered to the bereaved. It offers community to those who are isolated, and a space for the exploration of feelings and questions, aided by a facilitator with some insight and training in pastoral care.

Not every church will be able to do this on their own – and perhaps they do not need to. A few years after I started work in Hoddesdon, the parish was joined with two neighbouring parishes into a group ministry. Although we remained as four separate churches (one parish had two churches in it), with different church councils and leadership, there were areas where we could cooperate together. Bereavement support was an obvious example of this. Many churches have links – formal and informal – with neighbouring churches and I would hope that bereavement support groups would be able to work across more than one church community.

One of the hardest aspects of being a parish priest is that the time needed for good quality pastoral care is often squeezed out by the demands of the next meeting, or other preparation work that has to be done. As I reflect on my own funeral ministry, I am all too aware that pastoral care for the bereaved after the funeral has often suffered by the overwhelming busyness that can overtake me. I am so grateful to God that there were others in the church community who were able to come alongside the bereaved and continue that pastoral care. It seems to me to be a very good model of what the Body of Christ should be about – all of us exercising our gifts and different functions to support one another and proclaim the kingdom of God in word and deed.

Other services after the funeral

I remarked in an earlier chapter that there is a significant difference between burial and cremation concerning finality. When a person has been buried, their mortal remains have been effectively taken care of. Although some cultures have the practice of digging up the bones after at least ten years, in most cultures the dead body remains in the ground. However, when a person is cremated, that is not the end of the necessary procedures. There is a box of ashes that need to be dealt with by the family: further ritual needs to take place.

There is considerable confusion in people's minds as to what can be done with people's ashes. Cremated remains are often disposed of in a favourite place of the person who has died, which may be a hillside, or by a favourite lake, or on the pitch of the person's favourite football team. However, the Canons of the Church of England state that cremated remains should be disposed of in a churchyard or other burial ground or area of land so designated by the bishop, or at sea – no other option is given.[50] It does not answer the question of whether ashes can be disposed of elsewhere as long as church ministers are not involved. However, local authorities – and indeed football teams – are becoming increasingly concerned about the practice of scattering ashes on land belonging to them.

There will be occasions when the family approaches the church to ask if their loved one's ashes can be interred in the churchyard or local cemetery. In many churches now, churchyards have been officially closed – only ashes can be interred there if there is a designated Garden of Remembrance. Where there is such a garden, the ashes can be placed in an unmarked plot within the garden. Two things should be made clear to the family about this:

1. The ashes must be interred in the ground. They are not scattered around the churchyard, or underneath a favourite tree or in a rose bed: they must be placed in the ground.

---

50. The Canons of the Church of England B38 4(b).

2. No permanent memorial can be placed within the garden. This is difficult for people and contrasts with the situation in a cemetery. There, each plot of cremated remains is marked with a headstone or other marker, but in a Garden of Remembrance in a churchyard, no such marker is allowed. This often is very hard for families, and it should be certainly be made clear to them before the interment of ashes goes ahead.

When a family does want the church minister to inter the ashes, there is another opportunity to offer a brief service at the graveside, sharing with them the love of God. Often these services are very brief – little more than a short reading from the Psalms or elsewhere, some prayers and a time of silence. When the service follows fairly shortly on from the funeral, that is often enough. The interment of ashes is usually attended only by immediate family, and a short time of silence gives them the space that they need.

However, there are occasions where, pastorally, we should offer something more to the family. Sometimes, the family needs to remember their loved one in a formal, ritual way. They may want particular readings, or the opportunity to listen to a favourite piece of music. It may be appropriate to start the service in the church building itself rather than simply meeting in the Garden of Remembrance or cemetery to have the opportunity to sit and reflect together and then move outside for the final part of the service. Symbolic actions such as the release of a helium balloon, or even a dove, act as powerful gestures full of meaning, and can often help young children engage with the service.

I am wary of too many rituals immediately following a death. I think it can be exhausting for the family to have to go through a number of big services, and my tendency where the interment of ashes follows on within a few weeks of the person's death is to keep that service very brief and to allow silence to predominate. However, where there has been a greater distance from the person's death to the interment – and some people keep their loved one's ashes for several years before deciding what to do with them – it can be important to mark the final interment with greater ritual.

Annual services of remembrance

A ritual that has assumed increasing importance for people in recent years has been an annual service of remembrance. Roman Catholic churches and high Anglican churches in this country have led the way on this in their observation of All Souls' Day, on 2 November, which follows immediately on from All Saints' Day the previous day. All

Souls is a time when the Church has traditionally remembered 'the faithful departed' – those Christian people who are now numbered among the Church Triumphant in death, alongside the Church Militant in life.

I am reminded of the insights of Hippolytus, the third-century Church Father who I mentioned in Chapter 1, who saw the church as a ship on a stormy sea. But also on the sea making their way to port is the community of the faithful departed. On All Souls' Day we commemorate our fellow travellers, knowing that they make their way in peace, even as we go through trouble and danger.

One practical outworking of All Souls' Day has been the establishment of annual remembrance services to which are invited those people who have suffered bereavement over the previous year. Often these services are also attended by members of the congregation who have also lost husbands or wives, or other loved ones – sometimes many years previously. Nonetheless, the remembrance service offers people a chance to remember once more in a ritual context, and to give thanks for the person's life.

There are a number of practical issues to consider when offering a service of remembrance.

1. Consider carefully what the best time of year would be to observe it. I have written about the service in the context of an observation of All Souls' Day, but this may not be the right time of year for your church. If your church is not one where such Saints' days are observed, there may well be good reason to put it on at another time of year. Furthermore, it is likely that the majority of the people you invite to the service from the bereaved whose family funerals you have conducted will have no notion of All Souls' Day.

   From the point of view of society, a service around All Souls' Tide can work well because of the links that are now made in this country between November and Remembrance. The fact that this service will normally fall on the week before Remembrance Sunday keeps consistency in people's minds.

   However, there are good reasons to think about another time of day. These services are traditionally held in the late afternoon, when it is already getting dark and, where a good proportion of the likely congregation are retired and amongst the old, and it is not a time of day when they will want to leave their homes. Some churches hold the service of remembrance in the summer for precisely this reason – it is much easier for older people to come to the service.

   Another time of year when a remembrance service works well is in January. Although there are still the problems of dark and

wet evenings, psychologically it feels significant for families to mark a new year with remembering the pain of the old year, but in some way placing it in God's hands. There is a desire at such services at that time of year to look forward with hope as well as looking back with thanksgiving.
2. The use of symbolic gesture in a service of remembrance seems particularly important. Often at these services the opportunity is offered to come forward to light a candle. I know that, for many bereaved families, this is the central focus of the service. The family wants to be able to acknowledge that the light of their loved one's love lives on: and as Christian ministers, it is a good opportunity to point to Christ, the Light of the World, who shines in the darkest corners of our grief.
3. Don't forget to serve a good tea afterwards! Refreshments after a church service is not, of course, a new idea, but somehow following a remembrance service, it feels particularly important. People want to talk about the person whom they have remembered that day, and it is vital that the church provides people from their pastoral team, or members of the congregation who have good pastoral skills, to listen to those stories.

Conclusion

At the heart of the reason for good pastoral care is the insight that was raised at the very beginning of this book: the dead are not simply gone. They live on in another place and one day we will be reunited with our loved ones. In the light of this, it is right to continue to care for those whose family members have died, to find ways to remind them of this insight and to help them continue to remember them. This is not morbid or preventing people from 'moving on'; it is simply a recognition that those whom we love and see no longer are still part of us.

If the church is able to encourage people to do this, I think paradoxically it will help people have a healthy relationship with their dead. Some people may fear that I am suggesting that we should keep communication with the dead, but this is certainly not the case. The Bible makes it clear that we should not attempt to do this through mediums or spirit diviners (see, for example, Leviticus 19:31). However, I think one of the motivating forces that drives people to seek their dead out in this way is society's insistence that they should move on and leave their dead behind. Those whom we love are always part of us, even when they live in another place beyond us, and the Church should help people acknowledge that ongoing kinship.

Part 2
Resources

Introduction
Bible readings
Hymns
Other music
Prayers
Other readings
Readings for annual services of remembrance

Introduction

The second section of this book is devoted to providing liturgical resources that can be used at a funeral. It is divided into a number of sections:

1. Bible passages and readings: some of these passages can be used as single verses at appropriate points during the service; others work better as the Bible reading set for the service.
2. Hymns.
3. Prayers: these include prayers of confession, prayers of intercession and prayers of commendation.
4. Music to listen to: this includes pieces traditionally seen as 'religious' and pieces not seen as religious.
5. Other readings.

Part 3 of the book contains a number of templates for different services: these templates include funerals for children as well as adults, and also offer suggested orders of service for individual and annual collective memorial services.

The greatest change in content that has taken place in funerals over the last 20 years is how they have become much more tailored to the individual circumstances. Any list of resources, therefore, can only be limited – there will always be other music and readings that a grieving family has come across and would like incorporated into the service. A wise pastor will not try to impose a standard list of readings or hymns on a family. However, if this list can be used as a starting point to offer some suggestions, it will have achieved its objective.

Bible readings

Throughout the funeral service is the opportunity to read passages of the Bible: in the opening words as the coffin is brought into the church, in the reading of a Psalm together in place of a hymn, in the main Bible reading for the service, in words spoken at the time of committal.

The Psalms offer particularly rich resources for reading during a funeral – so many of them cry out to God in lament, and we would do well to recover some of these in the way we conduct funerals.

Those taking funerals will have their own preferences as to the version of Scripture to use. Sometimes it will be important for a family that the Authorised or King James Version is used. It is very easy to dismiss this version as archaic and unable to communicate to a modern world, but there are still many people who remember the power of its cadences and associate it still with the true words of Scripture. Familiarity is very important at a funeral, and if the words of the King James Version are familiar and comforting, that is a very good reason to use it.

Of course, with the plethora of different Bible versions available, I am aware that the King James Version is becoming less familiar, and there can be good reason to rely on the clarity of a modern translation.

Opening sentences
Words of hope

The eternal God is your refuge, and underneath are the everlasting arms. (*Deuteronomy 33:27, NKJV*)

You show me the path of life. In your presence there is fullness of joy; in your right hand are pleasures for evermore. (*Psalm 16:11*)

God is our refuge and strength, a very present help in trouble. (*Psalm 46:1*)

The steadfast love of the Lord never ceases, his mercies never come to an end; they are new every morning; great is your faithfulness. (*Lamentations 3:22-3*)

As a mother comforts her child, so will I comfort you, [says the Lord]. (*Isaiah 66:13*)

Blessed are those who mourn, for they will be comforted. (*Matthew 5:4*)

[Jesus said,] 'Truly I tell you, today you will be with me in Paradise.' (*Luke 23:43*)

God so loved the world that he gave his only Son, so that everyone who believes in him may not perish but may have eternal life. *(John 3:16)*

Jesus said . . . 'I am the resurrection and the life. Those who believe in me, even though they die, will live, and everyone who lives and believes in me will never die.' *(John 11:25-6)*

I am convinced that neither death, nor life, nor angels, nor rulers, nor powers, nor things present, nor things to come, nor height, nor depth, nor anything else in all creation, will be able to separate us from the love of God in Christ Jesus our Lord. *(Romans 8:38-9, amended)*

Words of sorrow

In you, O Lord, I seek refuge; do not let me ever be put to shame; in your righteousness deliver me. *(Psalm 31:1)*

Will you not revive us again, so that your people may rejoice in you? Show us your steadfast love, O Lord, and grant us your salvation. *(Psalm 85:6-7)*

I, O Lord, cry out to you; in the morning my prayer comes before you. O Lord, why do you cast me off? Why do you hide your face from me? *(Psalm 88:13-14)*

Out of the depths I cry to you, O Lord. Lord, hear my voice!
Let your ears be attentive to the voice of my supplications!
If you, O Lord, should mark iniquities, Lord, who could stand?
But there is forgiveness with you, so that you may be revered.
I wait for the Lord, my soul waits, and in his word I hope;
my soul waits for the Lord more than those who watch for the morning, more than those who watch for the morning.
O Israel, hope in the Lord!
For with the Lord there is steadfast love, and with him is great power to redeem.
It is he who will redeem Israel from all its iniquities. *(Psalm 130)*

By the rivers of Babylon – there we sat down and there we wept . . . How could we sing the Lord's song in a foreign land? *(Psalm 137:1, 4)*

We brought nothing into the world, so that we can take nothing out of it. The Lord gave and the Lord has taken away; blessed be the name of the Lord. *(1 Timothy 6:7; Job 1:21b)*

Psalms to read together

As I say in the section of hymn resources, where there is a small congregation, it can work well to read a psalm together. The following psalms are well known and are often read together as part of a funeral service:

- Psalm 23
- Psalm 27
- Psalm 42
- Psalm 46
- Psalm 90
- Psalm 103:8-18
- Psalm 121
- Psalm 130

Bible readings
Old Testament and Apocrypha
Job 19:23-7: I know that my Redeemer lives.

Ecclesiastes 3:1-8, 11, 14: For everything there is a season.

Song of Songs 8:6-7: Set me as a seal upon your heart.

Isaiah 53: The suffering servant.

Isaiah 61:1-3: The Spirit of the Lord is upon me . . . to comfort all who mourn.

Lamentations 3:22-33: The steadfast love of the Lord never ceases.

Wisdom of Solomon 3:1-9: The souls of the righteous are in the hands of God.

Wisdom of Solomon 4:7-11, 13-15: The righteous will be at rest.

Sirach (or Ecclesiasticus) 38:16-23: Let your tears fall for the dead.

New Testament: Gospel readings
Matthew 5:1-12: The Beatitudes.

Matthew 11:25-30: Come to me, all you that are weary.

Matthew 25:31-46: The parable of the sheep and the goats.

Mark 10:13-16: Let the little children come to me.

Mark 15:33-9: Mark's account of the death of Jesus.

Luke 12:35-40: The coming of the Son of Man.

Luke 24:13-35: The road to Emmaus.

John 6:35-40: I am the bread of life.

John 11:17-27: I am the resurrection and the life.

John 12:23-8: Unless a grain of wheat falls into the ground and dies, it remains just a single grain.

John 14:1-6, 27: In my Father's house are many dwelling-places.

John 20:11-18: The risen Jesus appears to Mary Magdalene.

New Testament: Epistle readings

Romans 5:5-11: Hope does not disappoint us.

Romans 8:18-25: All creation waits for the future glory.

Romans 8:31-9: Nothing can separate us from the love of God.

Romans 14:7-12: Whether we live or die, we are the Lord's.

1 Corinthians 15:20-8: Christ has been raised, the first fruits of those who have died.

1 Corinthians 15:51-7: Death has been swallowed up in victory.

2 Corinthians 4:7-15: We carry in our mortal bodies the death of Christ.

2 Corinthians 4:16–5:10: Our inner nature is renewed day by day.

Ephesians 3:14-21: May we know the love of Christ that surpasses knowledge.

Philippians 3:7-16, 20-1: Our citizenship is in heaven.

Philippians 4:4-9: The peace of God will guard our hearts and minds.

1 Thessalonians 4:13-18: We shall be with the Lord forever.

2 Timothy 2:8-13: If we have died with Christ, we shall also live with him.

1 John 3:1-3: See what love God has given us.

Revelation 7:9-17: The multitudes worship in heaven.

Revelation 21:1-7: A new heaven and a new earth.

Scripture verses at the committal

Where the committal takes place at a separate service from the funeral – at the crematorium or cemetery, where the main service has taken place in church – it is helpful to include further verses from the Psalms or other Scriptures, which can be taken from the list above or from the following list:

A mortal, born of woman, few of days and full of trouble; comes up like a flower and withers, flees like a shadow and does not last. (*Job 14:1*)

The Lord is merciful and gracious,
slow to anger and abounding in steadfast love.
He will not always accuse,
nor will he keep his anger for ever.
He does not deal with us according to our sins,
nor repay us according to our iniquities.
For as the heavens are high above the earth,
so great is his steadfast love towards those who fear him;
as far as the east is from the west,
so far he removes our transgressions from us.

As a father has compassion for his children,
so the Lord has compassion for those who fear him.
For he knows how we were made,
he remembers that we are dust.
As for mortals, their days are like grass;
they flourish like a flower of the field;
for the wind passes over it, and it is gone,
and its place knows it no more.
But the steadfast love of the Lord is from everlasting to everlasting
on those who fear him,
and his righteousness to children's children,
to those who keep his covenant
and remember to do his commandments. (*Psalm 103:8-18*)

Come, you that are blessed by my Father, inherit the kingdom prepared for you from the foundation of the world. (*Matthew 25:34*)

This is the will of him who sent me, that I should lose nothing of all that he has given me, but raise it up on the last day. (*John 6:39*)

Our citizenship is in heaven, and it is from there that we are expecting a Saviour, the Lord Jesus Christ. (*Philippians 3:20*)

Jesus Christ . . . the firstborn of the dead . . . to him be glory and dominion forever and ever. (*Revelation 1:5-6*)

The Nunc Dimittis (Song of Simeon)

Where I use the Nunc Dimittis at a funeral, I always use it in the version printed in the Church of England *Book of Common Prayer*, which is the form printed below, or the King James Version. This is because it is the version that is nearly always familiar in my own context. I tend only to use it with committed church members, who would be more likely to know the old version. There may be justification sometimes for using a modern translation, but, like using the modern version of the Lord's Prayer, it is worth thinking carefully before doing so!

> Lord, now lettest thou thy servant depart in peace, according to thy word.
> For mine eyes have seen thy salvation,
> which thou hast prepared before the face of all people;
> to be a light to lighten the Gentiles, and to be the glory of thy
> people Israel.   *Luke 2:29-32*

Blessings and endings

Most of the letters of the New Testament end with a blessing on the recipients of the letter, and many can be adapted as below to be used in public worship.

[Jesus said,] 'I am with you always, to the end of the age.' (*Matthew 28:20*)

Now to God who is able to strengthen you, according to my gospel and the proclamation of Jesus Christ, according to the revelation of the mystery . . . now disclosed . . . to the only wise God, through Jesus Christ, to whom be the glory for ever! Amen. (*Romans 16:25,27*)

Maranatha! Our Lord, come! (*1 Corinthians 16:22*)

The grace of the Lord Jesus Christ, the love of God, and the communion of the Holy Spirit be with all of you. (*2 Corinthians 13:13*)

Peace be to the whole community, and love with faith, from God the Father and the Lord Jesus Christ. Grace be with all who have an undying love for our Lord Jesus Christ. (*Ephesians 6:23-4*)

Now to him who is able to keep you from falling, and to make you stand without blemish in the presence of his glory with rejoicing, to the only God our Saviour, through Jesus Christ our Lord, be glory, majesty, power, and authority, before all time and now and for ever. Amen. (*Jude 24-5*)

Hymns

I have divided these hymns into a number of different categories – metrical psalms, songs of mourning, hymns of pilgrimage and hymns of praise. There is, of course, overlap between the categories, but I have placed any individual hymn in the section where it seems to fit most naturally.

Hymn choices are very personal, and often with a funeral, the overriding factor is what hymns the family actually knows. For those with a good knowledge of hymns, here are some suggestions.

Psalms

With a small congregation, it may be best to read a psalm together. Psalms 23, 46, 90, 121 or 130 all work very effectively for this.

Hymn choices include:

'All people that on earth do dwell' from the Geneva Psalter (Tune: Old hundredth) (Psalm 100)

'I to the hills will lift mine eyes' from the Scottish Psalter (Tune: French (Dundee) (Psalm 121)

'Let us with a gladsome mind' by John Milton (Tune: Monkland) (Psalm 136)

'O God our help in ages past' by Isaac Watts (Tune: St Anne) (Psalm 90)

'The King of Love' by H. W. Baker (Tune: Dominus Regit Me or St Columba) (Psalm 23)

'The Lord's my shepherd' from the Scottish Psalter (Tune: Crimond or Brother James' air) (Psalm 23)

'The Lord's my shepherd' by Stuart Townend (Psalm 23)

'God is our strength and refuge' by Richard Bewes (Tune: Dambusters' march) (Psalm 46)

Songs of sorrow and ending

'Abide with me' by H. F. Lyte (Tune: Eventide)

'Be still my soul' by K. von Schlegel, translated by Jane Borthwick (Tune: Finlandia)

'Calm me, Lord' by David Adam

'From the falter of breath' by John L. Bell and Graham Moule (Tune: Iona boat song)

'God that madest earth and heaven' by R. Heber and R. Wheatley (Tune: Ar Hyd y Nos)

'Going home' by Michael Forster (Tune: New world)

'Now the day is over' by Sabine Baring-Gould (Tune: Eudoxia)

'Now the green blade riseth' by John Macleod Campbell Crum (Tune: Noel nouvelet)

'Rock of Ages' by Augustus Toplady (Tune: Petra or Toplady)

'Saviour again to thy dear name we raise' by J. Ellerton (Tune: Ellers)

'The day thou gavest' by J. Ellerton (Tune: St Clement)

Songs of pilgrimage

'Blessed be your name' by Beth and Matt Redman

'Dear Lord and Father of mankind' by John Greenleaf Whittier (Tune: Repton)

'Father, hear the prayer we offer' by Maria Willis (Tune: Sussex or Marching)

'Guide me O thou great Redeemer' by William Williams (Tune: Cwm Rhondda)

'In heavenly love abiding' by Anna Waring (Tune: Penlan)

'Lord for the years' by Timothy Dudley-Smith (Tune: Lord of the years)

'Make me a channel of thy peace' by Sebastian Temple

'O Jesus, I have promised' by John Ernest Bode (Tune: Day of Rest/Wolvercote/Hatherop Castle)

'One more step along the world I go' by Sydney Carter (Tune: Southcote)

'The old rugged cross' by George Bennard (Tune: The old rugged cross)

'Who would true valour see' by John Bunyan (Tune: Monk's Gate)

Songs of praise

'All things bright and beautiful' by Cecil Frances Alexander (Tune: All things bright or Royal Oak)

'Amazing grace' by John Newton (Tune: Amazing grace)

'Be thou my vision' traditional Irish, translated by Mary Byrne (Tune: Slane)

'Glory to thee, my God, this night' by Thomas Ken (Tune: Tallis' Canon)

'Great is thy faithfulness' by Thomas O. Chisholm (Tune: Faithfulness)

'How great thou art' by Stuart K. Hine (Tune: How great thou art)

'Love divine' by Charles Wesley (Tune: Love divine or Blaenwern)

'Morning has broken' by Eleanor Farjeon (Tune: Bunessan)

'Mine eyes have seen the glory' by Julia Ward Howe (Tune: Battle Hymn of the Republic)
'Now thank we all our God' by Martin Rinkart (Tune: Nun danket)
'Praise my soul' by H. F. Lyte (Tune: Praise my soul)
'Thine be the glory' by E. L. Budry, translated by Richard Hoyle (Tune: Maccabeus)

There are a number of hymns that have been written – often to well-known hymn tunes – that are particularly appropriate at the death of a child. Here are some suggestions. The words to these hymns are on the following pages :
'Christ be beside me' by Alister Bull (Tune: Bunessan)
'Fleetingly known yet ever remembered' by an unknown author (Tune: Bunessan)
'Thank you for the gifts we treasure' by Dorothy Moore Brooks (Tune: Praise my soul)
'There is a place' by John L. Bell (Tune: Dunblane)
'We cannot care for you the way we wanted' by John L. Bell (Tune: Jennifer)

Words to hymns suggested for use in children's funerals

'Christ be beside me' by Alister Bull

Christ be beside me, Christ be before me.
Christ be behind me, King of my heart.
Christ be within me, Christ be below me,
Christ be above me, never to part.

Christ of our loved ones, carry our burdens,
hear all our questions, anger and pain.
Heal the deep hurting, comfort our grieving,
clear our confusion, let hope remain.

Christ in the new day, Christ at its setting,
seeking his blessing, knowing his will.
Hearts that are aching, in his arms resting,
gently he whispers, 'Peace to you still.'

'Fleetingly known' by an unknown author

Fleetingly known yet ever remembered,
these are our children now and always,
these whom we see not, we will forget not,
morning and evening, all of our days.

Lives that touched our lives, tenderly briefly,
now in the one light living always,
named in our hearts now, safe from all harm now,
we will remember all of our days.

As we recall them silently name them,
open our heads, Lord, now and always.
Grant to us grieving, love for the living,
strength for each other all of our days.

Safe in your peace, Lord, hold these your children.
Grace, light and laughter grant them each day.
Cherish and hold them till we may know them,
when to your glory we find our way.

'Thank you for the gifts we treasure' by Dorothy Moore Brooks

Thank you for the gifts we treasure,
past and present, seen, unseen.
People, places, life's experience,
faith and doubt, our hopes and dreams.
Come with light and come with comfort,
shine in us through all our days.

Thank you for the wealth of memories
of our children, still so dear.
Tears and laughter, joys and sorrows,
make their presence feel so near.
Come with light and come with comfort,
shine in us through all our days.

Thank you for the care of others
as we walk unchartered ways;
hands that hold ours through the sorrow,
shining light in darkest days.
Come with light and come with comfort,
shine in us through all our days.

Thank you for the hope that fills us
as we journey from this place
to that time where all our questions,
tears and longing find deep peace.
Come with light and come with comfort,
shine in us through all our days.

'There is a place' by John L. Bell

There is a place prepared for little children,
those we once lived for, those we deeply mourn,
those who from play, from learning and from laughter
cruelly were torn.

There is a place where hands which held ours tightly
now are released beyond all hurt and fear,
healed by that love which also feels our sorrow
tear after tear.

There is a place where all the lost potential
yields its full promise, finds its lost intent;
silenced no more, young voices echo freely
as they were meant.

There is a place where God will hear our questions,
suffer our anger, share our speechless grief.
Gently repair the innocence of loving
and of belief.

Jesus, who bids us to be like little children,
shields those our arms are yearning to embrace,
God will ensure that all are reunited;
there is a place.

'We cannot care for you the way we wanted' by John L. Bell

We cannot care for you the way we wanted,
or cradle you or listen for your cry,
but separated as we are by silence,
love will not die.

We cannot watch you grow into childhood
and find a new uniqueness every day;
but special as you would have been among us,
you still will stay.

We cannot know the pain or the potential
which passing years would summon or reveal,
but for that true fulfilment Jesus promised
we hope and feel.

So through the mess and anger, grief and tiredness,
through tensions which are not reconciled,
we give to God the worship of our sorrow
and our dear child.

Other music

It is with regard to considering what music to have that funerals today have become most idiosyncratic, most particular to the person who has died. Favourite pieces are chosen – Chapter 5 contains a list of the ten most popular choices in 2009 according to The Co-operative Funeralcare – but it is when choosing music that the family will often find ways of connecting with the character and unique memories of the person who has died. So I have left a church to 'I am the very model of a modern major-general' for a man who was a keen member of the local amateur dramatics society; I have listened to the bagpipes play 'Dream Angus' for a patriotic Scottish woman; I have listened to countless songs sung by Michael Bublé and Eva Cassidy when everybody knew that their loved one was a big fan of their music.

Music has the power to evoke memory more emphatically than almost any other medium. That is why I think it can be so helpful for a family to have a favourite piece of music played. Often families will want a particular item to be played as the coffin is brought into church or taken out, but as I discussed in Chapter 5, there can be good pastoral and liturgical reasons to include a particular piece of music in the middle of the service.

Sometimes it is possible to bring in a choir to sing an anthem as part of the service. If the service is in a church, there may a parish choir available to sing. The practical difficulty that often has to be overcome, of course, is that most funerals take place during the working day when many choir members will be at work. However, if it is possible for the choir to sing – or for a choir to be brought in – this can transform a funeral service. The choir may well be able to sing an anthem, a setting of 'God be in my head' or the 'Nunc Dimittis' as the loved one is commended into God's hands.

Some clergy are more comfortable when any such music is played on the organ, or by the pianist leading the music in the service. Undoubtedly, music played live is generally to be preferred to a CD or MP3 recording, but there are occasions when a recorded version is to be preferred. If the person who has died was a big fan of Dolly Parton, for example, with the best will in the world, it will not be the same simply to have the organist play the tune of 'Nine to five' – the family will want to hear Dolly singing!

It is important to consider the laws of copyright in this regard. When the service is at the crematorium or in the cemetery, it may well be that the crematorium will have paid for an annual licence from the

Performing Rights Society (PRS) to play recordings of music that is still under copyright: it is possible therefore to offer reassurance to a family that recordings of particular music – legally obtained, of course! – will not break the laws of copyright by being played as part of the service.

However, whilst many churches will have a similar licence that they use in respect of modern worship songs, issued by the CCLI (Christian Copyright Licensing International), they may well not be covered by the licence for secular songs and music. The guidelines issued by the PRS, however, mean that churches would not normally need to obtain a licence. The PRS uses its discretion to say that it does not charge the fees that would normally arise when the performance event is a private family function. An obvious example of this would be a funeral in church – though it would also cover weddings as well.

The Co-operative Funeralcare list of favourite songs to be played at a funeral offers a good starting point for what music to consider:

1. 'My way' by Frank Sinatra or Shirley Bassey
2. 'Wind beneath my wings' by Bette Midler or Celine Dion
3. 'Time to say goodbye' by Andrea Boccelli and Sarah Brightman
4. 'Angels' by Robbie Williams
5. 'Somewhere over the rainbow' by Eva Cassidy
6. 'You raise me up' by Boyzone, Westlife or Josh Grobin
7. 'My heart will go on' by Celine Dion
8. 'I will always love you' by Witney Houston
9. 'You'll never walk alone' by Gerry and the Pacemakers
10. 'Unforgettable' by Nat King Cole

However, if the purpose of the music is to allow the family to call to mind their own particular memories, perhaps knowing what other people are likely to choose is less important than choosing something that means something to them and to the family.

Many people would feel profoundly uncomfortable listening to any of the above tracks in a church, though for a crematorium it may not feel so bad. We do find it easier to accept classical music which can be played on an organ as more fitting for the occasion – whether or not that organ music was originally written with a religious context in mind. The following are some suggestions for classical music, many of which can be played on the organ, if it is not deemed appropriate to listen to a recording of them.

Tomaso Albinoni	'Adagio in G minor'
Johann Sebastian Bach	'Sheep may safely graze'
	'Jesu, joy of man's desiring'
	'Toccata and Fugue in D minor'

Samuel Barber	'Adagio for strings' (also the music for a setting of 'Agnus Dei')
Claude Debussy	'Claire de lune'
Edward Elgar	'Nimrod' from *Enigma Variations*
Gabriel Fauré	'Pie Jesu' *or* 'In Paradisum' from Requiem
César Franck	'Panis Angelicus'
Georg Frideric Handel	'Hallelujah Chorus', 'He shall feed his flock' *or* 'I know that my Redeemer liveth' from *The Messiah*
Wolfgang Amadeus Mozart	'Ave Verum Corpus'
Pachelbel	'Canon in D'
John Williams	'Cavatina'

All these options are suggestions only and illustrations of the sort of the music that is often popular. Here, more than for any other element of the service, it is important to listen to the choices that the family wants.

Prayers

When I suggest to bereaved families that, as part of our prayers, we will say the Lord's Prayer together, there is always an acknowledgement of the rightness of doing this. If death raises questions of the future and what happens after it, using the words of a prayer that is still familiar to many from childhood provides reassurance and comfort. It is also a reminder of the importance of prayer in funeral services. Even when families use civil celebrants, many will want to say the words of the Lord's Prayer during the service as an acknowledgement of the need to reach out beyond human understanding in making sense of what has happened with the death of a loved one.

This section offers a number of suggestions for prayers. For some Christians, the idea of using any prayer which has been written by somebody else, other than the Lord's Prayer, is anathema – prayer should be the spontaneous response of the individual heart to their loving heavenly Father. In this case, this section will not contain anything that is helpful. For other Christians, there is reassurance in using other people's prayers, and it is to be hoped that this section can offer some helpful resources.

Opening prayers and confessions

God of all mercies,
you make nothing in vain
and love all that you have made.
Comfort us in our grief,
and console us by the knowledge of your unfailing love,
through Jesus Christ our Lord. Amen
Church of England, Common Worship Funeral Order, alternative prayer

O God, who brought us to birth
and in whose arms we die,
in our grief and shock,
comfort and contain us;
embrace us with your love,
give us hope in our confusion,
and grace to let go into new life,
through Jesus Christ. Amen
Church of England, Common Worship Funeral Order, alternative prayer

God our comforter,
you are our refuge and strength,
a helper close at hand in times of trouble.
Help us so to hear your word
that our fear may be dispelled,
our loneliness eased,
and our hope awakened.
May your Holy Spirit lift us above our sorrow
to the peace and light of your constant love;
through Jesus Christ our Lord. Amen
Methodist Worship Book Funeral Order

(Following the death of a child)
Loving God,
we are lost and it is dark;
we are hurting but feel nothing;
we know but we cannot take it in.
Be a light to our footsteps,
a balm to our wounds,
and lead us to your truth;
through Jesus Christ,
your dead but risen Son. Amen
Derek Browning[51]

Confessions

Forgiving God,
in the face of death we discover
how many things are still undone,
how much might have been done otherwise.
Redeem our failure.
Bind up the wounds of past mistakes.
Transform our guilt to active love,
and by your forgiveness make us whole.

God our Redeemer,
you love all that you have made,
you are merciful beyond our deserving.
Pardon your servant's sins,
acknowledged or unperceived.
Help us also to forgive as we pray to be forgiven,
through him who on the cross
asked forgiveness for those who wounded him.
Through Jesus Christ our Lord. Amen
Scottish Episcopal Church Revised Common Liturgy

---

51. Taken from Fraser Smith, *Arranging a Funeral: A Book of Resources*, London: SPCK, 2006.

The following prayers, using the format of the *Kyrie Eleisons* (Lord, have mercy), use from the Psalms:

Remember, O Lord, your compassion and love, for they are everlasting.
Lord, have mercy.
Lord, have mercy.

Remember not the sins of my youth or my transgressions,
but think on me in your goodness, O Lord,
according to your steadfast love.
Christ, have mercy.
Christ, have mercy.

O keep my soul and deliver me;
let me not be put to shame, for I have put my trust in you.
Lord, have mercy.
Lord, have mercy.

Out of the depths, I cry to you;
Lord, hear my voice.
Lord, have mercy.

If you should mark what is done amiss;
who may abide it?
Christ, have mercy.
Christ, have mercy.

Trust in the Lord, for with him there is mercy,
for with him there is ample redemption.
Lord, have mercy.
Lord, have mercy.
Church of England Common Worship Funeral Order

Prayers of intercession

Included amongst the prayers during the service should be the Lord's Prayer. My own preference is always to use the traditional words since they are still the most familiar. However, if an order of service is being printed, it is good to print the words out these days – they are familiar, but people are embarrassed when they can't remember them. There may well come a time when people are no more familiar with the traditional words than the modern words, in which case it may be worth using the modern words. Until that time comes, I would err on the side of tradition.

Our Father, who art in heaven
hallowed be thy name.
Thy kingdom come, thy will be done
on earth as it is in heaven.
Give us this day our daily bread,
and forgive us our trespasses,
as we forgive those
who trespass against us.
Lead us not into temptation,
but deliver us from evil,
for thine is the kingdom,
the power and the glory
For ever and ever. Amen

Our Father in heaven,
hallowed be your name.
Your kingdom come, your will be done,
on earth as in heaven.
Give us today our daily bread,
and forgive us our sins
as we forgive those who sin against us.
Lead us not into temptation,
but deliver us from evil,
for the kingdom,
the power and the glory are yours,
now and forever. Amen

God of mercy, Lord of life,
you have made us in your image
to reflect your truth and light:
we give you thanks for N,
for the grace and mercy *he/she* received from you,
for all that was good in *his/her* life,
for the memories we treasure today.
[*Especially we thank you . . .*]

You promised eternal life to those who believe.
Remember for good this your servant N
as we also remember *him/her*.
Bring all who rest in Christ
into the fullness of your kingdom
where sins have been forgiven
and death is no more.

Your mighty power brings joy out of grief
and life out of death.
Look in mercy on [. . . *and*] all who mourn.
Give them patient faith in times of darkness.
Strengthen them with the knowledge of your love.

You are tender towards your children
and your mercy is over all your works.
Heal the memories of hurt and failure.
Give us the wisdom and grace to use aright
the time that is left to us here on earth,
to turn to Christ and follow in his steps
in the way that leads to everlasting life.

God of mercy, entrusting into your hands all that you have made,
and rejoicing in our communion with all your faithful people,
we make our prayers through Jesus Christ our Saviour. Amen
Church of England Common Worship Funeral Service

Father of all,
we pray for those whom we love, but see no longer.
Grant them your peace;
let light perpetual shine upon them;
and in your loving wisdom and almighty power
work in them the good purpose of your perfect will;
through Jesus Christ our Lord. Amen
Methodist Worship Book Funeral Order

Almighty God,
Father of all mercies and giver of all comfort;
deal graciously we pray with those who mourn,
that casting all their care on you,
they may know the consolation of your love;
through Jesus Christ our Lord. Amen

God of all consolation,
in your unending love and mercy for us,
you turn the darkness of death into the dawn of new life.
Show compassion to your children in their sorrow.
Be our refuge and strength
to lift us from the darkness of this grief,
to the peace and light of your presence.
Your son, our Lord Jesus Christ,
by dying for us, conquered death
and by rising again, restored life.

May we then go forward eagerly to meet him,
and after our life on earth
be reunited with our brothers and sisters,
where every tear will be wiped away.
Author unknown[52]

Support us, O Lord,
all the day long of this troublous life,
until the shades lengthen, and the evening comes,
the busy world is hushed, the fever of life is over, and our work is done.
Then, O Lord, in your mercy grant us a safe lodging,
a holy rest and peace at the last;
through Jesus Christ our Lord. Amen
Cardinal John Henry Newman

God of all consolation,
open our hearts to your word,
so that, listening to it, we may comfort one another,
finding light in times of darkness
and faith in times of doubt.
We ask this through Jesus Christ our Lord. Amen
Roman Catholic Church Order of Christian Funerals

For our *brother/sister* N, let us pray to the Lord Jesus Christ, who said, 'I am the resurrection and the life.'
Lord, you consoled Martha and Mary in their distress. Draw near to us who mourn for N, and dry the tears of those who weep.
Hear us, Lord.
You wept at the grave of Lazarus your friend; comfort us in our sorrow.
Hear us, Lord.
You raised the dead to life; give to our *brother/sister* eternal life.
Hear us, Lord.
You promised paradise to the thief who repented; bring our *sister/brother* to the joys of heaven.
Hear us, Lord.
Our *brother/sister* was washed in baptism and anointed with the Holy Spirit; give *him/her* fellowship with all your saints.
Hear us, Lord.
S/he was nourished with your body and blood; grant *him/her* a place at the table in your heavenly kingdom.
Hear us, Lord.

---

52. Taken from Smith, *Arranging a Funeral*.

Comfort us in our sorrows at the death of N; let our faith be our consolation, and eternal life our hope.
Silence is kept.
Grant, O Lord, to all who are bereaved, the spirit of faith and courage, that we may have strength to meet the day to come with steadfastness and patience; not sorrowing without hope, but in remembrance of your great goodness, and in the expectation of eternal life with those we live. And this we ask in the name of Jesus Christ our Saviour. Amen
Lisa Belcher Hamilton [53]

We give back to you, O God, those whom you gave to us.
You did not lose them when you gave them to us,
and we do not lose them by their return to you.
Your dear Son has taught us that life is eternal
and love cannot die,
so death is only a horizon
and a horizon is only the limit of our sight.
Open our eyes to see more clearly and draw us close to you,
that we may know that we are nearer to our loved ones, who are with you.
You have told us that you are preparing a place for us;
prepare us also for that happy place,
that where you are we many also be always,
O dear Lord of life and death. Amen
William Penn

Bring us, O Lord our God, at our last awakening
into the house and gate of heaven,
to enter into that gate and dwell in that house,
where there shall be no darkness or dazzling,
but one equal light;
no noise or silence, but one equal music;
no fears or hopes, but one equal possession;
no ends or beginnings, but one equal eternity;
in the habitations of thy glory and dominion,
world without end. Amen
John Donne

---

53. Taken from Lisa Belcher Hamilton, *For those we love but see no longer*, London, SPCK:2001.

A prayer suitable at a cremation service

As the flames of earth consume our mortality,
so in the fullness of time the flame of your love
may remake us eternally in the glory and stature of Christ
who alone is the light of the world,
the light that no darkness can end,
who, with you and the Holy Spirit,
is God for ever and ever. Amen
Douglas Davies

Prayers of commendation and ending

This prayer can obviously also be used with modern language, as appropriate.

Give rest, O Christ, to thy servant with thy saints:
where sorrow and pain are no more;
neither sighing but life everlasting.
Thou only art immortal, the creator and maker of man:
and we are mortal formed from the dust of the earth,
and unto earth shall we return:
for so thou didst ordain,
when thou created me saying:
'Dust thou art and unto dust shalt thou return.'
All we go down to the dust;
and weeping o'er the grave we make our song:
Alleluia, alleluia, alleluia.

Into your keeping, O merciful God,
we commend your servant N.
Receive *her/him* into the arms of your mercy,
into the joy of everlasting peace,
and into the glorious company of the saints in light;
through Jesus Christ our Lord. Amen
Methodist Worship Book Funeral Order

Into your hands, Father of mercies,
We commend our *brother/sister N*,
in the sure and certain hope
that, together with all who have died in Christ,
he/she will rise with him on the last day.
Merciful Lord,
turn towards us and listen to our prayers:
open the gates of paradise to your servant

and help us who remain
to comfort one another with assurances of faith,
until we all meet in Christ
and are with you and with our *brother/sister* for ever.
We ask this through Jesus Christ our Lord. Amen
Roman Catholic Church funeral rite

God be in my head, and in my understanding;
God be in mine eyes, and in my looking;
God be in my mouth, and in my speaking;
God be in my heart, and in my thinking;
God be at mine end, and at my departing.
Sarum Primer

I have printed the next prayer in traditional language, because of its familiarity in this form to generations of Church of England worshippers at Evensong. Given that it is most familiar in this form, I think it is justified to leave it in traditional language even in a modern language service.

Lord, now lettest thou thy servant depart in peace according to thy word.
For mine eyes have seen thy salvation,
which thou hast prepared before the face of all people;
to be a light to lighten the Gentiles and to be the glory of thy
people Israel.
Nunc Dimittis or Song of Simeon from Luke 2:29-32

The following prayer is often used at the time of death, but it could also be used at the funeral as a symbolic handing over to God, which is, after all, what the commendation is.

Go forth upon your journey from this world, O Christian soul, in peace;
in the name of God the Father who created you;
in the name of Jesus Christ who died for you;
in the name of the Holy Spirit who strengthens you.
In communion with the blessèd Virgin Mary
and all the blessèd saints;
with the angels and archangels
and all the heavenly host.
May your portion this day be in peace
and your dwelling in the city of God.
Amen

N, may Christ give you rest in the land of the living
and open for you the gates of paradise;
may he receive you as a citizen of the kingdom,
and grant you forgiveness of your sins:
for you were his friend. Amen

The following two commendations may be particularly suitable for babies and young children.

Into the darkness and warmth of the earth – we lay you down.
Into the sadness and smiles of our memories – we lay you down.
In the cycle of living and dying and rising again – we lay you down.
May you rest in peace, in fulfilment, in loving.
May you run straight home into God's embrace. Amen
The Iona Community

Child of my flesh,
bone of my bone,
wherever you go, I go,
wherever you live, I will live.
As you go into the mystery of life before us,
may you be at peace;
that in God's good time
we may be together in peace.
SANDS (Stillbirth & Neonatal Death Society)

Blessings

Deep peace of the running wave to you,
deep peace of the flowing air to you,
deep peace of the quiet earth to you,
deep peace of the shining stars to you,
deep peace of the Son of Peace to you.
May the road rise to meet you;
may the wind be always at your back;
may the sun shine warm upon your face;
may the rains fall softly upon your fields.
Until we meet again,
may God hold you in the hollow of his hand.
Traditional Celtic blessing

Now unto him who is able to keep you falling,
and to present you faultless before his presence
with exceeding joy;
to the only wise God our Saviour, be glory and majesty,
power and authority,
now and forever. Amen
Taken from Jude 24-5

The hand of the Lord is gentle,
and though we cannot understand,
he comforts us with his gentle hand.

The hand of the Lord is loving,
and though it seems our hope is gone,
his love brings strength to carry on.

The hand of the Lord brings healing,
and though our hearts are filled with pain,
his healing hand brings peace again.

And may the blessing of God, Father, Son and Holy Spirit, be with you and those whom you love and those who love you, now and forever more. Amen
Fraser Smith[54]

---

54. Taken from Smith, *Arranging a Funeral*.

Other readings

It is fairly common at funerals nowadays for there to be various non-biblical readings as part of the service, whether or not the service is in church or conducted by a church minister. In Chapter 3, I reflected on some of these readings and expressed a concern that many of them seek to deny the reality of death or offer false hope at a time of grief. For that reason, I have omitted from this section two of the most popular readings that are used at funerals – 'Death is nothing at all' by Henry Scott Holland, and 'Do not stand at my grave and weep' by Mary Elizabeth Fry.

However, there are many poems and readings that can be used at a funeral which help a family through this time. I set out key considerations in Chapter 1 when deciding how to assess a reading, and suggest that these might be useful things to bear in mind:

- What significance do they have for the dead – either in calling the person to mind or in sending them on their way to God?
- Do they help the bereaved come to terms with a loved one's death?
- Do they give expression to the grief felt at a funeral?
- Do they provide hope for the future?

I think all of the following readings help with the process.

'Funeral blues' by W. H. Auden (1907–1973)

This poem was made famous, of course, by the film *Four Weddings and a Funeral*. It certainly expresses the grief that is often so present at a funeral.

Stop all the clocks, cut off the telephone,
prevent the dog from barking with a juicy bone,
silence the pianos and with muffled drum
bring out the coffin, let the mourners come.

Let aeroplanes circle moaning overhead
scribbling on the sky the message He Is Dead,
put crepe bows round the white necks of the public doves,
let the traffic policemen wear black cotton gloves.

He was my North, my South, my East and West,
my working week and my Sunday rest,
my noon, my midnight, my talk, my song;
I thought that love would last for ever: I was wrong.

The stars are not wanted now: put out every one;
pack up the moon and dismantle the sun;
pour away the ocean and sweep up the wood,
for nothing now can ever come to any good.

'The ship' by Bishop Charles Brent (1862–1929)

Bishop Brent was an American bishop in the Philippines. This piece reminds us that our earthly perspective on death is partial: if life continues beyond the grave, others welcome as we say goodbye.

I am standing on the seashore.
A ship sails in the morning breeze and starts for the ocean.
She is an object of beauty and I stand watching her
till at last she fades on the horizon and someone at my side says,
'She is gone.'

Gone! Where? Gone from my sight – that is all.
She is just as large in the masts, hull and spars as she was when I saw her,
and just as able to bear her load of living freight to its destination.
The diminished size and total loss of sight is in me,
not in her.

And just at the moment when someone at my side says,
'She is gone,' there are others who are watching her coming, and other voices
take up a glad shout: 'There she comes' – and that is dying.

'i carry your heart with me' by e. e. cummings (1894–1962)

This poem is often also used at weddings. Perhaps we should not be surprised at that: what we remember most at funerals, and what gives us hope, is love.

i carry your heart with me (i carry it in
my heart) i am never without it (anywhere
i go you go, my dear; and whatever is done
by only me is your doing, my darling)
i fear
no fate (for you are my fate, my sweet) i want
no world (for beautiful you are my world, my true)
and it's you are whatever a moon has always meant
and whatever a sun will always sing is you

here is the deepest secret nobody knows
(here is the root of the root and the bud of the bud
and the sky of a tree called life; which grows
higher than soul can hope or mind can hide)
and this is the wonder that's keeping the stars apart

i carry your heart (i carry it in my heart)

'On joy and sorrow' by Kahlil Gibran (1883–1935)

Gibran was a Lebanese-born poet and writer who moved with his family to the USA when he was 12. His best-known work is *The Prophet*, which is a series of philosophical reflections on different aspects of life. His works are often also read at weddings. The nearness of joy and sorrow is a reminder that at their heart is love.

Then a woman said, 'Speak to us of joy and sorrow.'
And he answered:
Your joy is your sorrow unmasked.
And the selfsame well from which your laughter rises was oftentimes filled with your tears.
And how else can it be?
The deeper that sorrow carves into your being, the more joy you can contain.
Is not the cup that holds your wine the very cup that was burned in the potter's oven?
And is not the lute that soothes your spirit the very wood that was hollowed with knives?
When you are joyous, look deep into your heart and you shall find it is only that which has given you sorrow that is giving you joy.
When you are sorrowful, look again in your heart, and you shall see that in truth you are weeping for that which has been your delight.
Some of you say, 'Joy is greater than sorrow,' and others say, 'Nay, sorrow is the greater.'
But I say unto you, they are inseparable.
Together they come, and when one sits alone with you at your board, remember that the other is asleep upon your bed.
Verily you are suspended like scales between your sorrow and your joy.
Only when you are empty are you at standstill and balanced.
When the treasure-keeper lifts you to weigh his gold and his silver, needs must your joy or your sorrow rise or fall.

'If I should go' by Joyce Grenfell (1910–1979)

Joyce Grenfell is best known for her comedy routines. However, this poem, with its acknowledgement that 'parting is hell', offers a helpful insight into grief. It is often used at funerals.

If I should die before the rest of you,
break not a flower nor inscribe a stone,
nor, when I'm gone, speak in a Sunday voice,
but be the usual selves that I have known.
Weep if you must:
parting is hell.
But life goes on.
So sing as well.

'Because he lived' by Edgar A. Guest (1881–1959)

Edgar Guest was a popular American poet at the turn of the twentieth century. He wrote more than 11,000 poems, which were published in newspapers and heard on his weekly radio show in the 1930s. This poem reflects well the desire to bring to mind memories of a person at their funeral.

Because he lived, next door a child
to see him coming often smiled,
and thought him her devoted friend
who gladly gave her coins to spend.

Because he lived, a neighbour knew
a clump of tall delphiniums blue
and oriental poppies red
he'd given for a flower bed.

Because he lived, a man in need
was grateful for a kindly deed
and ever after tried to be
as thoughtful and as fine as he.

Because he lived, ne'er great or proud
or known to all the motley crowd,
a few there were whose tents were pitched
near his who found their lives enriched.

'You can shed tears' by David Harkins (1959–)

This poem was read at the funeral of Queen Elizabeth the Queen Mother. It is often uncredited, but I believe it was written by David Harkins. It can be read for a man or a woman by the simple substitution of 'she' for 'he', etc., as appropriate.

You can shed tears that he is gone,
or you can smile because he has lived.

You can close your eyes and pray that he will come back,
or you can open your eyes and see all that he has left.

Your heart can be empty because you can't see him,
or you can be full of the love that you shared.

You can turn your back on tomorrow and live yesterday,
or you can be happy for tomorrow because of yesterday.

You can remember him and only that he is gone,
or you can cherish his memory and let it live on.

You can cry and close your mind, be empty and turn your back,
or you can do what he would want: smile, open your eyes, love and go on.

'The life that I have' by Leo Marks (1920–2001)

It is said that Marks wrote this poem following the death of his girlfriend in 1943. He handed it to the French spy, Violette Szabo, as an encrypted message. The poem was used in the film of her life, *Carve her Name with Pride*, in 1958.

The life that I have
is all that I have.
And the life that I have
is yours.

The love that I have
of the life that I have
is yours and yours and yours.

A sleep I shall have,
a rest I shall have,
yet death will be but a pause.

For the peace of my years
in the long green grass
will be yours and yours and yours.

'Remember' by Christina Rossetti (1830–1894)

Many of Christina Rossetti's poems deal with the sadness of death, loss and ill health, yet there is a simplicity and directness about her poetry that prevents her being maudlin. This poem is one of the best known of hers, and is read often at funerals.

Remember me when I am gone away,
gone far away into the silent land;
when you can no more hold me by the hand,
nor I half turn to go yet turning stay.
Remember me when no more day by day
you tell me of our future that you planned:
only remember me; you understand
it will be late to counsel then or pray.
Yet if you should forget me for a while
and afterwards remember, do not grieve:
for if the darkness and corruption leave
a vestige of the thoughts that once I had,
better by far you should forget and smile
than that you should remember and be sad.

'When I must leave you' by Helen Steiner Rice (1900–1981)

Helen Steiner Rice is well known for her inspirational verse, and her thoughts have been widely reproduced in greetings cards. This poem comes close to denying grief, though in speaking so much of it, acknowledges its presence.

When I must leave you for a little while –
please do not grieve and shed wild tears
and hug your sorrow to you through the years.
But start out bravely with a gallant smile;
and for my sake and in my name
live on and do all things the same.
Feed not your loneliness on empty days,
but fill each waking hour in useful ways.

Reach out your hand in comfort and in cheer,
and I in turn will comfort you and hold you near;
and never, never be afraid to die,
for I am waiting for you in the sky!

'Footprints in the sand' by Mary Stevenson (1922–1999)

This is a much-loved reading, and generally ascribed to an anonymous author. Mary Stevenson had it copyrighted in 1984 in the USA and was able to show before her death that a handwritten copy that she wrote in 1939 was authentic and pre-dated any other copy of the reading.

One night I dreamed I was walking along the beach with the Lord.
Many scenes from my life flashed across the sky.
In each scene I noticed footprints in the sand.
Sometimes there were two sets of footprints,
other times there was one set of footprints.

This bothered me because I noticed
that during the low periods of my life,
when I was suffering from
anguish, sorrow or defeat,
I could see only one set of footprints.

So I said to the Lord,
'You promised me, Lord,
that if I followed you,
you would walk with me always.
But I have noticed that during
the most trying periods of my life
there has only been one
set of footprints in the sand.
Why, when I needed you most,
have you not been there for me?'

The Lord replied,
'The times when you have
seen only one set of footprints,
is when I carried you.'

'I pray today' by Rabindranath Tagore (1861–1941)

This is an extract from a poem entitled 'Gitanjali', by the Bengali poet, Tagore.

I pray today
in all earnestness
with all my heart and soul
for those whose hands
have reared me
and held me close,
for those who have caressed
and eased my pain
and borne the suffering with me;
for those whose hearts
have wept in grief
and yet
sung happy songs to me;
for those who show
the patience rare
and help me
to keep my cool;
for those who dwell
in my bruised heart
and keep me wrapped
with the warmth of their love.
How can any harm
come to me,
when I am protected
with an armour of love?

'Crossing the bar' by Alfred, Lord Tennyson (1809–1892)

The imagery of death as a journey over the sea is a popular one and harks back to the pagan world where the dead were carried over the underworld river to Hades. This poem reminds us of the Pilot who will steer us on our journey home.

Sunset and evening star,
and one clear call for me!
And may there be no moaning of the bar,
when I put out to sea.

But such a tide as moving seems asleep,
too full for sound and foam,
when that which drew from out the boundless deep
turns again home.

Twilight and evening bell,
and after that the dark!
And may there be no sadness or farewell,
when I embark.

For tho' from out our bourne of Time and Place
the flood may bear me far,
I hope to see my Pilot face to face
when I have crost the bar.

'In memoriam' by Alfred, Lord Tennyson (1809–1892)

Tennyson wrote this epic poem after the death of his dear friend Arthur Hallam in 1833. It was written over 17 years and consists of 131 stanzas and an epilogue. I have just included Stanza 130 here.

Thy voice is on the rolling air;
I hear thee where the waters run;
thou standest in the rising sun,
and in the setting thou art fair.

What art thou then? I cannot guess;
but tho' I seem in star and flower
to feel thee some diffusive power,
I do not therefore love thee less.

My love involves the love before;
my love is vaster passion now;
tho' mix'd with God and Nature thou,
I seem to love thee more and more.

Far off thou art, but ever nigh;
I have thee still, and I rejoice;
I prosper, circled with thy voice;
I shall not lose thee tho' I die.

'Dandelion clock' by an unknown author

This is a poem that Dorothy, my wife, placed in a collection of resources that she had put together for her work, but we have been unable to trace it or find it in any other collection. In a time of chaos and uncertainty, it offers hope and peace.

Hope is a dark elusive child,
curled in the womb,
cradled in our arms.
It can be lost,
disappear,
blown on the wind like a dandelion clock.

Its going,
its ebbing away
leaves us
grieving,
empty,
hopeless.

'But' is a hopeful word.

But even as the gossamer
powder puff
disintegrates,
the seeds are carried
to cling to distant crevices.
As it recedes,
it reseeds,
to grow again.

God, giver of peace,
grow hope within and around us.
God of steadfast love,
never leave us hopeless.

'Let me go' by an unknown author

One source suggests that this poem was written by Edgar A. Guest, but I have not been able to verify that. I think it combines well the need to grieve for someone, but to do so with hope that God has drawn them to himself.

When I come to the end of the road
and the sun has set for me,
I want no rites in a gloom-filled room.
Why cry for a soul set free?
Miss me a little, but not for long,
and not with your head bowed low.
Remember the love that once we shared.
Miss me, but let me go.
For this is a journey we all must take,
and each must go alone.
It's all part of the Master's plan,
a step on the road to home.

When you are lonely and sick at heart,
go to the friends we know.
Laugh at all the things we used to do,
miss me, but let me go.

'God gives and God takes away' by Lindon Jane Vogel

I have not been able to find any further information about Lindon Vogel, but this brief sentiment encapsulates an important truth that undermines the 'death is nothing at all' school of readings, or indeed a tendency at some Christian services that we should have no reason to be sad.

God gives life,
and God takes life away.
And the taking away is so terribly painful
because what he gives is so very good.

Readings particularly suitable for the death of a child

'Act of farewell'

We came across this simple reading from a leaflet given to us by SANDS (Stillbirth and Neonatal Death Society), when our son Matthew was stillborn. SANDS does a wonderful job in supporting families going through the shock of the death of a newborn child, in offering resources and practical support groups.

Child of my flesh,
bone of my bone,
wherever you go, I go,
wherever you live, I will live.
As you go into the mystery of life before us,
may you be at peace,
that in God's good time,
we may be together in peace.

'Gone too soon' by Buz Kohan

This was written as a song with Larry Grossman in 1983 and made most famous when Michael Jackson sang it at the inauguration of President Bill Clinton in memory of a friend who had died of AIDS.

Like a comet blazing across the evening sky,
gone too soon.

Like a rainbow fading in the twinkling of an eye,
gone too soon.

Shiny and sparkly, splendidly bright,
here one day, gone one night.

Like the loss of sunlight on a cloudy afternoon,
gone too soon.

Like a castle built upon a sandy beach,
gone too soon.

Like a perfect flower that is just beyond your reach,
gone too soon.

Born to amuse, to inspire, to delight,
here one day, gone one night.

Like a sunset dying with the rising of the moon,
gone too soon.

'Bring my child back to me' by Barbara Patterson

In my previous church, we held an annual service for those whose children had died, at any age, in any circumstances, however long ago. It was always well attended and this poem was often used.

Whisper, whisper, wind in the woods,
bring back my child, here where he stood,
let him laugh, let him shout, let him giggle with glee,
wind in the woods, bring my child back to me.

Silence of morning, dew on the grass,
give me peace in my soul, let this time pass,
let my child sit beside me, let the two of us be,
silence of morning, bring my child back to me.

Middle of night, so dark and so still,
let me relax and remember at will,
let my child in my thoughts drift forever to see,
middle of night, bring my child back to me.

Sunrise and sunset, beginning and end,
give me a day with my child, my friend,
we'll run on the beach, we'll play in the sea,
sunrise, sunset, bring my child back to me.

Memories, memories here in my head,
don't ever leave me, even though my child's dead,
keep him alive, keep him strong, keep him free,
memories of mine, bring my child back to me.

'Too soon' by Mary Yarnall

For parents who have experienced the death of a child, the sense of loss at what might have been is overwhelming. They have no memories with which to console themselves – but they still have love.

This was a life that had hardly begun.
No time to find your place in the sun.
No time to do all you could have done,
but we loved you enough for a lifetime.

No time to enjoy the world and its wealth.
No time to take life down off the shelf.
No time to sing the songs of yourself,
though you had enough love for a lifetime.

Those who live long endure sadness and tears,
but you'll never suffer the sorrowing years.
No betrayal, no anger, no hatred, no fears,
just love – only love – in your lifetime.

'The other side of midnight' by an unknown author

This poem gives hope that death is not simply the end. Of course, the Christian message is that the 'other place' is not simply in our heart – it is with God and in his.

The other side of midnight,
not so many miles away,
enwrapped in hazy memories
our newborn babies play.

Tended safe by unknown hands
in a place we cannot see,
our babies live another life
from earthly cares set free.

From the other side of midnight
they visit us in sleep,
caress our grief with infant hands
when in our dreams we weep.

Though in our darkest days we seem
a million miles apart,
in time we learn that other place
is really in our heart.

The other side of midnight,
at last we learn to see,
our babies live within us
cradled in our memory.

Readings for annual services of remembrance

In addition to the readings listed above, the following are particularly appropriate at annual services of remembrance.

'I remember, I remember' by the Centering Corporation

The Centering Corporation is an American organisation, set up in 1977, to offer support to the bereaved. This poem reflects on the seasons and the memories that each evokes.

In the spring, when the first crocus
pokes its head tentatively out of the frozen ground,
I think of you and I remember . . .
I remember.

In the summer, when the glaring heat
wilts the rose petals and paints unsightly cracks in the ground,
I think of you and I remember . . .
I remember.

In the autumn, when the trees are ablaze
in the glory of fall and my shoes make crackling sounds as I walk,
I think of you and I remember . . .
I remember.

And in the winter, when I stand at my window
to watch a blizzard whirl snow around my grief and loneliness,
then, too, I think of you and I remember . . .
yes, I remember.

'Sometimes' by Marsha Updike

This poem will feel most true for a service some time after the funeral and death of a loved one – that is why I think it works best at an annual memorial service.

Sometimes,
memories are like the rain showers
sprinkling down upon you,
catching you unaware.
And then they are gone,
leaving you warm and refreshed.

Sometimes,
memories are like thunderstorms,
beating down upon you,
relentless in their downpour.
And then they will cease,
leaving you tired and bruised.

Sometimes,
memories are like shadows
sneaking up behind you,
following you around.
Then they disappear,
leaving you sad and confused.

Sometimes,
memories are like comforters,
surrounding you with warmth,
luxuriously abundant.
And sometimes they stay,
wrapping you in contentment.

'Remember me' by an unknown author

It seems sad that so many of these poems and reflections are unattributed.

To the living, I am gone.
To the sorrowful, I will never return.
To the angry, I was cheated.
To the happy, I am at peace.
To the faithful, I have never left.
I cannot speak, but I can listen.
I cannot be seen, but I can be heard.
So as you look in awe at a mighty forest and its grand majesty,
remember me.
Remember me in your heart, your thoughts and your memories.
Of the times we cried, the battles we fought, and the times we laughed.
For if you always think of me, I will never have gone.

A litany of remembrance

I use this litany at our annual service of remembrance to which we invite all whose loved ones have died in the previous three years. As part of the service, they come forward to light a candle in the loved one's memory. Then we say this litany together, with the congregation joining in the words in bold. It, of course, picks up on the rhythm of the responses used on Remembrance Sunday to remember those killed in war.

In the rising of the sun and in its going down,
we will remember them.
We will remember them.
In the blowing of the wind and in the chill of winter,
we will remember them.
We will remember them.
In the opening of buds and in the rebirth of spring,
we will remember them.
We will remember them.
In the blueness of the sky and in the warmth of summer,
we will remember them.
We will remember them.
In the rustling of leaves and in the beauty of autumn,
we will remember them.
We will remember them.
In the beginning of the year and when it ends,
we will remember them.
We will remember them.
When we are weary and in need of strength
we will remember them.
We will remember them.
When we are lost and sick at heart,
we will remember them.
We will remember them.
When we have joys we yearn to share,
we will remember them.
We will remember them.
So long as we live, they too shall live,
for they are part of us,
and we will remember them.
We will remember them.

Part 3
Suggested orders of service

Suggested order of service for a funeral
Suggested order of service for a child's funeral
Suggested order of service for a vigil
Suggested order of service for an individual memorial service
Suggested order of service for the interment of ashes
Suggested order for an annual memorial service

Suggested order of service for a funeral

Many readers will have their own templates, and indeed may use a standard order of service as provided by their own denomination. The following order will in no way usurp that; it is simply provided to offer ideas that can be incorporated into your own order of service. As with all these templates, this section should be used in conjunction with the resources section, and other prayers and readings can be inserted where indicated.

This order envisages that the service will take place in church prior to going on to the crematorium or cemetery. Where that is not the case, the commendation will go straight into the words of committal and the blessing will be reserved until the end.

The minister meets the coffin at the church door or gate and walks in front of it, leading it in, speaking these opening sentences, or other words of sorrow, with family members and other mourners following the coffin.

Out of the depths, I cry to you, O Lord.
O Lord, hear my voice!
Let your ears be attentive
to the voice of my supplications!
If you, O Lord, should mark iniquities,
Lord, who could stand?
But there is forgiveness with you,
so that you may be revered.
I wait for the Lord, my soul waits,
and in his word I hope;
my soul waits for the Lord
more than those who watch for the morning
more than those who watch for the morning.
O Israel, hope in the Lord!
For with the Lord there is steadfast love,
and with him is great power to redeem.
It is he who will redeem Israel
from all its iniquities.
Psalm 130

The minister greets the people in his/her own words or as follows to remind them of the purposes of the funeral:

We are here today to mourn together the death of N,
to give thanks for *his/her* life and to comfort each other as we grieve.
We also gather to commend *him/her* to God and to remind ourselves of
the hope we have in Jesus;
and to commit N's body to be buried/cremated.

An opening prayer may be said:

O God, who brought us to birth
and in whose arms we die,
in our grief and shock,
comfort and contain us;
embrace us with your love,
give us hope in our confusion,
and grace to let go into new life;
through Jesus Christ. Amen

An opening hymn may be sung, or where the gathering is relatively small, a psalm may be said together.

The congregation should be seated after the hymn is sung.

Minister:

As we spend time calling to mind our memories of N through the tributes paid to *him/her*, and in quiet reflection, we know that amidst the memories of joy and thankfulness, there are also hard memories: times when we let *him/her* down, or times when *he/she* failed us. At the start of our service, let us offer to God the difficult memories, and hear his words of forgiveness.

Either or both of the following prayers may be said by the minister on behalf of the congregation:

Forgiving God,
in the face of death we discover
how many things are still undone,
how much might have been done otherwise.
Redeem our failure.
Bind up the wounds of past mistakes.
Transform our guilt to active love,
and by your forgiveness make us whole. Amen

God our Redeemer,
you love all that you have made,
you are merciful beyond our deserving.

Pardon your servant's sins,
acknowledged or unperceived.
Help us also to forgive as we pray to be forgiven,
through him who, on the cross,
asked forgiveness for those who wounded him,
through Jesus Christ our Lord. Amen

There then follows a tribute and/or non-biblical readings to call the person to mind. These will usually be given by family members and friends.

A second hymn may be sung. Alternatively, or in addition, a piece of music may be played – either live or a recorded version.[55]

A passage from the Bible is read.

A sermon is preached.

Prayers of intercession
The following prayers are based on Psalm 27 – space should be provided between each section to call to mind specific aspects of the person's life as appropriate, or to leave space for silence.

Minister:

Let us pray.
'The Lord is my light and my salvation . . . The Lord is the stronghold of my life.'
Let us give thanks for the life of N, for all *he/she* gave to us, for *his/her* life lived in the shelter and strength of God.

'Your face, O Lord, do I seek; do not hide your face from me.'
Remember N in your love and mercy as we also remember *him/her* – may *he/she* know your peace and presence in death, as *he/she* knew it in life.

'God will hide me in his shelter in the day of trouble; he will conceal me under the cover of his tent.'
We pray for those who mourn, remembering by name [. . .] Be not far from them, our God, and may they know your shelter in their troubles.

'One thing I asked of the Lord, that will I seek after: to live in the house of the Lord all the days of my life.'
We ask for strength to live in the light of eternity, putting our trust in God who is from everlasting to everlasting.

---

55. According to the Performing Rights Society, it is permissible to play a recorded version of a song or piece of music under copyright at a funeral without seeking copyright permission, or paying a fee – funerals are covered as private family events.

'Wait for the Lord; be strong, and let your heart take courage; wait for the Lord!' (v.14)
Amen

Minister:

Joining all our prayers and memories together, we say the word of the Lord's Prayer:

**Our Father, who art in heaven,
hallowed be thy name.
Thy kingdom come, thy will be done,
on earth as it is in heaven.
Give us this day our daily bread,
and forgive us our trespasses,
as we forgive those who trespass against us.
And lead us not into temptation,
but deliver us from evil,
for thine is the kingdom, the power and the glory,
For ever and ever. Amen**

A third hymn may be sung.
At the end of the hymn, the congregation remain standing for the commendation.

Minister:

Let us commend our *brother/sister*, N, to God, our merciful creator, redeemer and life-giver.
Give rest, O Christ, to your servant N with your saints:
where sorrow and pain are no more;
neither sighing but life everlasting.
You alone are immortal, creator and maker of all things:
and we are mortal formed from the dust of the earth,
and unto dust shall we return.
For so you ordained when you created us, saying:
'You are dust and unto dust shall you return.'
All of us go down to the dust;
yet weeping at the grave we make our song:
Alleluia, alleluia, alleluia.

The Nunc Dimittis or 'God be in my head' may be said or sung at this point in the service:

Lord, now lettest thou thy servant depart in peace according to
thy word.
For mine eyes have seen thy salvation,

which thou hast prepared before the face of all people;
to be a light to lighten the Gentiles and to be the glory of thy
people Israel.

OR

God be in my head, and in my understanding;
God be in mine eyes, and in my looking;
God be in my mouth, and in my speaking;
God be in my heart, and in my thinking;
God be at mine end, and at my departing.

Blessing

The hand of the Lord is gentle,
and though we cannot understand,
he comforts us with his gentle hand.

The hand of the Lord is loving,
and though it seems our hope is gone,
his love brings strength to carry on.

The hand of the Lord brings healing,
and though our hearts are filled with pain,
his healing hand brings peace again.

And may the blessing of God, Father, Son and Holy Spirit, be with you and those whom you love and those who love you, now and forever more. **Amen**

The coffin is then taken out of the church. The congregation may be encouraged to follow behind the coffin to the hearse and remain standing as the hearse drives away to the crematorium or cemetery. If the coffin is to be interred in the churchyard, the congregation should be encouraged to walk behind the coffin to the graveside.

Committal

As the coffin is carried into the crematorium chapel, or to the graveside, the minister should read these or other introductory sentences of hope:

God is our refuge and strength, a very present help in trouble. *(Psalm 46:1)*

The steadfast love of the Lord never ceases, his mercies never come to an end; they are new every morning; great is your faithfulness. *(Lamentations 3:22-3)*

'As a mother comforts her child, so will I comfort you,' says the Lord. *(Isaiah 66:13)*

[Jesus said,] 'Truly I tell you, today you will be with me in Paradise.'
(Luke 23:43)

God so loved the world that he gave his only Son, so that everyone who believes in him may not perish but may have eternal life.
(John 3:16)

'I am the resurrection and the life,' [says the Lord.] 'Those who believe in me, even though they die, will live, and everyone who lives and believes in me will never die.' *(John 11:25-6)*

I am convinced that neither death, nor life, nor angels, nor rulers, nor powers, nor things present, nor things to come, nor height, nor depth, nor anything else in all creation, will be able to separate us from the love of God in Christ Jesus our Lord. *(Romans 8:38-9, amended)*

The congregation may remain standing throughout the committal.

Minister:
The Lord is merciful and gracious,
slow to anger and abounding in steadfast love.
He will not always accuse, nor will he keep his anger for ever.
He does not deal with us according to our sins,
nor repay us according to our iniquities.
For as the heavens are high above the earth,
so great is his steadfast love towards those who fear him.
As far as the east is from the west,
so far he removes our transgressions from us.
As a father has compassion for his children,
so the Lord has compassion for those who fear him.
For he knows how we were made; he remembers that we are dust.
As for mortals, their days are like grass; they flourish like a flower of the field;
for the wind passes over it, and it is gone, and its place knows it
no more.
But the steadfast love of the Lord is from everlasting to everlasting on those who fear him, and his righteousness to children's children,
to those who keep his covenant and remember to do his commandments.
(Psalm 103)

Minister:
We have commended our *sister/brother*, N, to God's merciful keeping,
in sure and certain hope of the resurrection to eternal life
through our Lord Jesus Christ.
And we now commit *her/his* body to the ground / to be burnt.

Earth to earth, ashes to ashes, dust to dust.
The Lord bless *her/him* and keep *her/him*,
the Lord make his face to shine upon *her/him* and be gracious to *her/him*,
the Lord lift up the light of his countenance upon *her/him*
and give *her/him* peace.
Amen

The minister will then pronounce a final prayer:

And now unto him that is able to keep you from falling
and to present you faultless before the presence of his glory
with exceeding joy;
to the only wise God our Saviour,
be glory and majesty,
dominion and power,
both now and ever.
Amen

At a burial, mourners may be encouraged to place a flower or some earth on the coffin as a way of saying their own goodbye to the deceased.

The use of symbolic actions after a burial or a cremation could also be considered. Actions that are customarily used include the release of a dove or a balloon in the person's memory. Where children attend the committal, this is particularly popular.

Prayers and liturgy have been taken and adapted from *Church of England Common Worship* funeral order and *Roman Catholic Order of Christian Funerals*.

Suggested order of service for a child's funeral

As with every funeral, the funeral for a child needs to be prepared and crafted carefully and sensitively in partnership with the bereaved family. Perhaps one of the key things to bear in mind, however, is that there may be significant differences, in content at least, between the funerals of a tiny infant and that of a teenager. Appropriate hymns or music can be inserted at appropriate places in the service.

If individual flowers, photos or other special objects are to be laid on or around the coffin, or candles lit, I suggest that this happens early in the service – i.e. during an opening piece of music or first hymn.

Introduction
The minister should say words of welcome and comfort and which state what we are gathered to do.

Can a woman forget her nursing child, or show no compassion for the child of her womb? Even these may forget, yet I will not forget you. *(Isaiah 49:15)*

As a father has compassion for his children, so the Lord has compassion for those who fear him. *(Psalm 103:13)*

Opening prayer
God of love, the death of N brings an emptiness into our lives.
We are separated from *him/her*
and feel broken and bewildered.
As we gather to grieve and to give thanks for N,
Give us confidence that *he/she* is safe
and *his/her* life complete with you,
and bring us together at the last
to the wholeness and fullness of your presence in heaven,
where your saints and angels enjoy you for ever and ever. Amen

Readings

Tributes and personal memories (these may be written, spoken or visual)

Sermon

Music for reflection

Intercessions

Loving Father, from whom every family in heaven and on earth takes its name, we thank you for the place in our hearts that N held and still holds. We thank you for each precious memory of N: the first time we heard *she/he* was coming into the world, the first sight, sound of *him/her*, touch of *him/her*, our first cuddle with *him/her*,(*) for the many firsts in *his/her* life that spoke of a hope, a future and potential.(*) We give you thanks for *his/her* uniqueness and the love which *she/he* gave and received.

(*) *this phrase may not be appropriate if the child's life was hours or weeks*

We pray for N's parents who knew the joy of bringing *him/her* into the world only to experience the agony of *him/her* dying. We ask that you, the God who knows the searing pain of losing a beloved child, would comfort them in their sorrow and assure them that you will keep N safe in your arms until they meet again.

We pray for other members of N's family, *his/her* brothers and sisters [name them here] who will miss playing with *him/her*, as well as the joy of growing up together, for *his/her* grandparents, and all the family and friends who will miss N.

We pray that you will be gentle with this broken-hearted family. Give them hope when despair sets in, comfort when the tears flow, faithful friends when they are lonely, and courage when it is hard to take the next step. Be with them when other children reach landmarks that N will not reach. Help them to find creative, healing ways to keep N a part of their family life and collective memory.

We lay before you our feelings of hurt, bewilderment, disappointment, injustice, anger and grief that N should be taken from us so soon. We grieve at all the lost potential that has died with *him/her*. Bind up our wounds, give us faith that when your kingdom comes, such tragedies will have no place and that you will wipe away every tear from our eyes.

The Lord's Prayer:
Our Father, who art in heaven,
hallowed be thy name.
Thy kingdom come, thy will be done,
on earth as it is in heaven.
Give us this day our daily bread,
and forgive us our trespasses, as we forgive those who trespass against us.
Lead us not into temptation, but deliver us from evil,
for thine is the kingdom, the power and the glory,
for ever and ever. Amen

Commendation and committal

Heavenly Father, whose Son Jesus took little children into his arms and blessed them, we entrust this precious child, N, into your everlasting arms of love, for *he/she* is yours in death as in life. Gentle God, take and welcome *him/her* into your presence where there is no sorrow or pain, but perfect peace and unending love.

For a burial:

Into the darkness and warmth of the earth
we lay you down.
Into the sadness and smiles of our memories,
we lay you down.
Into the cycle of living and dying and rising again,
we lay you down.
May you rest in peace, in fulfilment, in loving.
May you run straight home in God's embrace.
Ruth Burgess

At either a burial or a cremation:

N, you shared your life with us;
God give eternal life to you.
You gave your love to us;
God give his deep love to you.
You gave your time to us;
God give his eternity to you.
You gave your light to us;
God give everlasting light to you.
Go upon your journey;
to love, light and life eternal.
David Adam

Act of farewell (to be read on behalf of the parents, or by them if they would like to)

Child of my flesh,
bone of my bone,
wherever you go, I go,
wherever you live, I will live.
As you go into the mystery of life before us,
may you be at peace.
That in God's good time
we may be together in peace.
SANDS (Stillbirth & Neonatal Death Society)

Blessing

Deep peace of the running wave to you.
Deep peace of the flowing air to you.
Deep peace of the quiet earth to you.
Deep peace of the shining stars to you.
Deep peace of the gentle night to you.
Moon and stars pour their healing light on you.
Deep peace of Christ,
of Christ the light of the world to you.
Deep peace of Christ to you.
Amen

Suggested order of service for a vigil

I find a service such as this one particularly helpful for a church member. It is not uncommon now for the family to want a private committal service prior to the funeral. Where that is the case, to hold a vigil the evening before the funeral service allows the person who has died to rest in the church building where they were a faithful member.

I have included the celebration of Communion as part of this service rather than in the main funeral service. This is because often at the funeral many people will be present – including close family members – who would not want to receive Communion. By placing the Communion in this smaller, more intimate setting, it provides hope and sustenance to the deceased's fellow church members and other Christian brothers and sisters.

As the coffin is received at the church door, the minister sprinkles it with water with these words:

In the waters of baptism, N died with Christ and rose with him to eternal life. As Christ went through the deep waters of death for us, so may he bring us to the fullness of resurrection life with N and all the redeemed.

The congregation is encouraged to follow behind the coffin and remain standing as the coffin is placed on the catafalque.

Symbols of the deceased person's faith are placed on the coffin, in silence or accompanied by the following words:

On the placing of a Bible:

In life, N cherished the Gospel of Christ. May Christ now greet *her/him* with these words of eternal life: Come, blessed of my Father!

On the placing of a cross:

Lord Jesus Christ, for the love of N and each one of us, you bore our sins on the cross.

On the lighting of the Paschal Candle, placed next to the coffin:

May the light of Christ, rising in glory, banish all darkness from our hearts and minds!

A hymn may be sung, or a psalm read together.

A Bible reading is read. If Communion is to be celebrated as part of the service, a Gospel reading should be used.

Silence may be kept, or a brief sermon given.

A time should be kept for prayer, either silently or led prayers of intercession.

The Lord's Prayer should be said either here or after the consecration of the Communion elements.

All should stand for the Peace.

Minister:
Jesus said, 'Peace I leave with you; my peace I give to you.
Not as the world gives do I give you.
Do not let your hearts be troubled, neither let them be afraid.' Alleluia.
The peace of the risen Lord be always with you.
And also with you.
All may exchange a sign of peace.

Holy Communion

Holy Communion should be celebrated according to the rites authorised by the tradition of the church where the service is held.

After they have been consecrated, the tokens of the bread and wine may be placed upon the coffin with these words:
Lord Jesus Christ, you sustain us through our lives with your body and blood in the Eucharistic meal. Be present with N as *she/he* travels the journey of death into the arms of God.

All baptised Christians are invited to receive communion.

The bread of heaven in Christ Jesus,
the cup of life in Christ Jesus.

After all have received communion, a prayer should be said together:
**Heavenly Father, in your Son Jesus Christ,
you have given us a true faith and a sure hope.
Strengthen this faith and hope in us all our days,
that we may live as those who believe in the communion of saints,
the forgiveness of sins and the resurrection to eternal life;
through Jesus Christ our Lord. Amen**

SUGGESTED ORDER OF SERVICE FOR A VIGIL

Minister:

On the night before Jesus died, after supper with his friends, they sang a hymn together, and departed into the darkness of the night. So we sing a hymn before departing in silence or resting in prayer, in the confusion of our grief, but with the hope of heaven in our hearts.

A hymn is sung and the congregation is encouraged to spend time in silence or leave silently when it is ended.

Prayers and liturgy have been taken and adapted from *Church of England Common Worship* funeral order and *Roman Catholic Order of Christian Funerals*.

Suggested order of service for an individual memorial service

Memorial services for individuals are now far more unusual than they used to be in this country, though it would seem that those deemed to be a celebrity will still have a memorial service as well as a funeral. The reason for their scarcity seems to be twofold:

1. Funerals – except for religions such as Islam or Judaism that require a rapid disposal of the body – often take place at least a week after the person has died. This gives more time to gather family and friends for the service, where previously they may not have been able to make it.
2. Funerals have become much more personal and focused on the life of the person who has died. Many of the tributes or readings which previously would have been heard only at a memorial service now find a place at the funeral itself.

A memorial service may also be known as a service of thanksgiving. It should, however, be distinguished from a service of thanksgiving that takes place on the same day as a burial or cremation but follows rather than precedes it. With this suggested order, I have in mind a service that takes place some time after the main funeral.

If such a memorial service is to be successful, I think the minister needs to think carefully to ensure that it goes beyond simply the spoken word. The presence of a coffin allows for symbolism to be drawn on as well as words, but a memorial service is denied that. Conversely, whilst an annual memorial service for all those who have died over the last year is a suitable place for the lighting of candles, that symbolism does not seem so obviously helpful with a single person's memorial service. Symbolic actions, such as the release of a balloon, or doves, may be appropriate, and it is important to give music an important role in the service.

Minister:

We look not to the things that are seen, but to the things that are unseen; for the things that are seen are transient, but the things unseen are eternal. Today we come together to remember before God our *brother/sister, N,* whom we love and see no longer, and to give thanks for *his/her* life.

A hymn may be sung.
All sit or kneel to pray.

Minister:

The gospel calls us to turn away from sin and be faithful to Christ.
Cast your burden upon the Lord
and he will sustain you.
In returning and rest
you shall be saved.
In quietness and trust
shall be your strength.
You raise the dead to life in the Spirit:
Lord, have mercy.
Lord, have mercy.
You bring pardon and peace to the broken in heart:
Christ, have mercy.
Christ, have mercy.
You bring light to those in darkness:
Lord, have mercy.
Lord, have mercy.

The minister pronounces God's forgiveness.

A tribute to the person who has died may be given. Non-biblical poems or prose passages may be read, and music that evokes the memory of the person who has died may be played. If there is a choir, an anthem may be sung; alternatively, recorded music may be used.[56]

A hymn may be sung.
A passage from the Bible is read.
A sermon is preached.

Prayers

A selection of prayers may be used in thanksgiving for the person who has died, in praying for comfort for the grieving and to remember before God our own mortality.

---

56. Personally, I take a fairly relaxed view as to how 'religious' the piece of music played is. Similarly, I do not mind a piece of prose or poetry that does not obviously have any religious inspiration. The point of these items at this point is to remind the congregation of the person who has died: they will be balanced in due course by Bible readings and the gospel message. What I find most irritating are clergy who allow classical music (whether or not they have any religious inspiration) but not other genres!

SUGGESTED ORDER OF SERVICE FOR AN INDIVIDUAL MEMORIAL SERVICE

Minister:

As our Saviour taught us, we say the words of the Lord's Prayer together:

**Our Father, who art in heaven,
hallowed be thy name.
Thy kingdom come, thy will be done,
on earth as it is in heaven.
Give us this day our daily bread,
and forgive us our trespasses, as we forgive those who trespass against us.
Lead us not into temptation, but deliver us from evil,
for thine is the kingdom, the power and the glory,
for ever and ever. Amen**

A hymn may be sung.

Concluding prayers:
Minister:

Grant to us, Lord God,
to trust you not for ourselves alone,
but also for those whom we love
and who are hidden from us by the shadow of death;
that, as we believe your power to raise from the dead,
so we may we trust your love to give eternal life to all who believe in him;
through Jesus Christ our Lord.
Amen

The love of the Lord Jesus draw you to himself,
the power of the Lord Jesus strengthen you in his service,
the joy of the Lord Jesus fill your hearts;
and the blessing of God Almighty,
the Father, the Son and the Holy Spirit,
be among you and remain with you always.
Amen

Prayers and liturgy have been taken and adapted from *Church of England Common Worship* memorial service and alternative prayers.

Suggested order of service for the interment of ashes

The need for a further service after a cremation highlights one of the differences between cremation and burial which has not really been thought about by those who create service orders. When a person is buried, that is the final thing to happen to them, but with cremation we are left with ashes which need to be disposed of. Most people do not want another service at this point, but when ashes are formally interred in a Garden of Remembrance or cemetery, a short act of remembrance and committal is appropriate.

My own personal view is that when the interment of ashes follows fairly soon after the funeral – within a few weeks – the service should be kept brief and use a minimum of words. The entire service can take place around the plot for interment. Often, it is only the immediate family who are present, and I feel that they should be allowed space for silence and their own memories and reflections.

Sometimes we are asked to inter ashes some time after the person has died – even, on occasion, a number of years. In these instances, particularly if there are to be a significant number of people attending the service, it is appropriate to incorporate some of the elements of a memorial service into the service and to start the service in church or in a chapel. Sometimes a symbolic action, such as the release of a balloon, or of doves, can speak powerfully to the family once the ashes have been interred.

The minister and family gather in the cemetery or Garden of Remembrance around the plot where the ashes are to be interred. The ashes may be placed in the ground prior to the beginning of the service, or at the point of committal.

Minister:
We meet together to bury the ashes of our *brother/sister*, N.
As we gather in faith we remember that, although our bodies return to dust, we shall be raised with Christ in glory. Let us rejoice in this promise as we hear God's word in Scripture.

A brief passage of Scripture, such as this one, or another, is used at this point.
Lord, you have been our dwelling place
in all generations.

HEAVEN'S MORNING BREAKS

Before the mountains were brought forth,
or ever you had formed the earth and the world,
from everlasting to everlasting you are God.
You turn us back to dust,
and say, 'Turn back, you mortals.'
For a thousand years in your sight
are like yesterday when it is past,
or like a watch in the night.
Psalm 90:1-4

If the ashes have not yet been placed in the ground, they are lowered at this point.

Minister:

We have commended our *brother/sister*, N, to God's everlasting love and care. We now return to the earth the ashes of *his/her* mortal body. May *he/she* rest in peace and rise in glory. Amen

As our Saviour has taught us, we pray together in the words of the Lord's Prayer:

All:
Our Father, who art in heaven,
hallowed be thy name.
Thy kingdom come, thy will be done,
on earth as it is in heaven.
Give us this day our daily bread,
and forgive us our trespasses,
as we forgive those who trespass against us.
And lead us not into temptation,
but deliver us from evil,
for thine is the kingdom, the power and the glory,
for ever and ever. Amen

Minister:

Heavenly Father, we thank you for those whom we love but see no longer.
As we remember N in this place,
hold before us our beginning and our ending,
the dust from which we come
and the death to which we move,
with a firm hope in your eternal love and purposes for us,
in Jesus Christ our Lord. Amen

SUGGESTED ORDER OF SERVICE FOR THE INTERMENT OF ASHES

Almighty God,
grant that we, with all who have trusted in you,
may be united in the full knowledge of your love,
and the unclouded vision of your glory;
through Jesus Christ our Lord. **Amen**

Blessing

Go out in the world
in the power of the Holy Spirit.
In all things and at all times
remember Christ is with you;
and the blessing of God Almighty,
the Father, the Son and the Holy Spirit,
be with you evermore. **Amen**

Prayers taken and adapted from *Church of England Common Worship*, The Burial of Ashes and *Methodist Worship Book*, A Service for the Burial of Ashes.

Suggested order for an annual memorial service

Many churches now hold annual memorial services, to which they invite all the families of those whose funerals church ministers have conducted over the last year, or the last few years, as well as members of their own congregation who wish to come and remember a loved one.

Memorial services are often very popular, and careful consideration should be given as to when they are held. Traditionally, they are held at All Souls' Tide – the Sunday nearest to 2 November – or in the afternoon of All Saints' Day (1 November). Whilst there is merit in this from a church point of view, if many of those coming are not regular members of the congregation, it is worth considering another time in the year. November can feel like a bleak month of the year, and as these services are often held in the late afternoon or early evening, older people may prefer not to come out after dark. Alternative times of year to consider include a summer month – though if lighting candles is part of the service, this is not so effective when it is light – or indeed January, when the symbolism of the new year speaks eloquently to people of looking forward with hope as well as looking back with thanksgiving for a life well lived.

Whatever time of year you choose, a memorial is one of those services where a good tea afterwards is absolutely vital! During this time, good pastoral work can be done and conversations about loved ones can flow.

The symbolic action of lighting a candle in memory of a loved one speaks extremely eloquently at a memorial service where many different families are gathered. A table should therefore be set up, offering the opportunity to light a candle. This may be a votive candle stand, or a table with a sand tray in which 3-inch candles can be placed and lit.

As people enter the church, they should be given a card on which they can write down the name of the loved one whom they are remembering in the service. There will be the opportunity to come forward and light a candle in the person's memory later in the service. Candles can also be provided at this point or when people come forward to light them.

Minister:

We look not to the things that are seen, but to the things that are unseen; for the things that are seen are transient, but the things unseen are eternal. Today we come together to remember before God those whom we love and are now unseen, and to give thanks for their lives.

A hymn may be sung.
All sit or kneel to pray.

Minister:

The gospel calls us to turn away from sin and be faithful to Christ.
Cast your burden upon the Lord
and he will sustain you.
In returning and rest
you shall be saved.
In quietness and trust
shall be your strength.
You raise the dead to life in the Spirit:
Lord, have mercy.
Lord, have mercy.
You bring pardon and peace to the broken in heart:
Christ, have mercy.
Christ, have mercy.
You bring light to those in darkness:
Lord, have mercy.
Lord, have mercy.

The minister pronounces God's forgiveness.

A psalm may be read together.

There is a reading from the Bible. It may be possible to use a non-biblical reading at this point.

A hymn may be sung.

A Bible reading will follow.

Sermon

All are now invited to come forward to light a candle in memory of loved ones who have died. The cards issued at the beginning of the service will be handed to a steward who will read out the names of those who are being remembered. The minister should then read out the names of any others who are being remembered in the service, whose families are unable to be present. Each candle lit represents one of the people remembered. The lights may be dimmed at this point in the service. After the names of those being remembered are read out, the minister leads a litany of remembrance.

In the rising of the sun and in its going down,
we remember them.
We remember them.
In the blowing of the wind and in the chill of winter,
we remember them.
We remember them.
In the blueness of the sky and in the warmth of summer,
we remember them.
We remember them.
In the rustling of leaves and in the beauty of autumn,
we remember them.
We remember them.
In the beginning of the year and when it ends,
we remember them.
We remember them.
When we are lost and sick at heart,
we remember them.
We remember them.
When we have joys we yearn to share,
we remember them.
We remember them.
So long as we live, they too shall live,
for they are part of us,
and we will remember them.

All sit or kneel for the prayers.

Almighty God, we bring you our thanks and praise today for those who shared our lives in times past. We thank you for times of happiness we had together, for the sorrows and difficulties we faced together, for all the experiences of both sunshine and shadow that we shared.

All: Almighty God, we thank you.

We thank you that our loved ones, who have gone from our sight, are in your keeping. Help us to leave them there in perfect trust. We thank you for those who have been a comfort and strength to us when we have felt down, for those whose love, care, encouragement and understanding we have so often taken for granted. We thank you for loyal friends and for those who have helped us bear our sorrows and overcome our fears.

All: Almighty God, we thank you.

We thank you that this life is not the end; that there is a place where all questions will be answered, all hopes realised, where we will meet again those whom we have loved and lost awhile. Grant to us, Lord God, to trust you not for ourselves alone but also for those whom we love who are hidden from us by the shadow of death.

All: Almighty God, we thank you.

By your grace, we pray, encourage our hearts and help us to remember that your peace is our comfort, your love is our strength, your presence is our joy.

All: Hear our prayer, through Jesus Christ our Lord. Amen

As our Saviour taught us, we say the words of the Lord's Prayer together:
**Our Father, who art in heaven,
hallowed be thy name.
Thy kingdom come, thy will be done,
on earth as it is in heaven.
Give us this day our daily bread,
and forgive us our trespasses, as we forgive those who trespass against us.
Lead us not into temptation, but deliver us from evil.
For thine is the kingdom, the power and the glory,
for ever and ever. Amen**

A hymn may be sung.

Blessing

May God, in his mercy, be with you in the darkness of your loss, and cause the light of hope, peace and eternal life to shine on you, and the blessing of God the Father, the Creator, God the Son, the Redeemer, and God the Holy Spirit, the giver of life, be with you now and always. Amen

Prayers and liturgy have been taken and adapted from the *Church of England Common Worship* memorial service and alternative prayers.

Bibliography

Books

Aquinas, Thomas, *Summa Theologica*, Vol II:II.

Balthasar, Hans Urs von, *Mysterium Paschale: The Mystery of Easter*, San Francisco: Ignatius Press, 1990.

Broyard, Anatole, *Intoxicated by my Illness and other writings on life and death*, New York: Ballantyne Books, 1993.

Brueggemann, Walter, *The Message of the Psalms*, Minneapolis: Augsberg Publishing House, 1984.

Carr, Wesley, *Brief Encounters: Pastoral Ministry through the Occasional Offices*, London: SPCK, 1985.

Davies, Douglas, *The Theology of Death*, London: T & T Clark, 2008.

Forster, E. M., *A Passage to India*, London: Penguin Classics, 2005.

Frankl, Viktor, E., *The Doctor and the Soul: From Psychotherapy to Logotherapy*, London: Souvenir Press Ltd, 2004.

Hamilton, Lisa Belcher, *For those we love but see no longer*, London: SPCK, 2001.

Long, Thomas, G., *Accompany them with Singing: The Christian Funeral*, Louisville: Westminster John Knox Press, 2009.

Lyall, David, *Integrity of Pastoral Care*, London: SPCK, 2001.

Lynch, Thomas, *The Undertaking Life: Studies from the Dismal Trade*, London: Vintage, 1998.

McGough, Roger, *Selected Poems*, London: Penguin, 2006.

Rochefoucauld, François de la, *Maxims* (1678) No. 26.

Sheppy, Paul, *Death Liturgy and Ritual, Vol 1*, Aldershot: Ashgate, 2003.

Smith, Fraser, *Arranging a Funeral: A Book of Resources*, London: SPCK, 2006.

Temple, William, *Nature, Man & God*, Edinburgh: T & T Clark, 1934.

Walter, Tony, *Funerals and How to Improve Them*, London: Hodder & Stoughton, 1990.

Walter, Tony, *The Revival of Death*, London: Routledge, 1994.

Westermann, Claus, *Praise and Lament in the Psalms*, Edinburgh: T & T Clark, 1981.

Wolsterstorff, Nicholas, *Lament for a Son*, Grand Rapids: Eerdmans, 1996.

Websites

County Celebrants Network see http://www.countycelebrantsnetwork.biz/A-Civil-Funeral-Ceremony.html

Good Funeral Guide, http://www.goodfuneralguide.co.uk/blog/

The Arbory Trust, www.arborytrust.org

The Association of Natural Burial Grounds, www.naturaldeath.org.uk

The Church of England, http://www.churchofengland.org

The Co-operative Funeralcare, www.co-operative.coop/Funeralcare

The Institute of Civil Funerals, www.iocf.org.uk

Other resources

Alternative Services, Second Series, London: Church of England Liturgical Commission, 1965.

Order of Christian Funerals: Rites of Committal, London: Burns & Oates, 1990, p.131.

Page, Maura, 'Grave Misgivings' in *Religion Today 3:* 1986 pp.7-9.

The Canons of the Church of England.

www.ingramcontent.com/pod-product-compliance
Lightning Source LLC
Chambersburg PA
CBHW051351070526
44584CB00025B/3720